The

Currency Carousel

The

Currency Carousel

A New Era in Monetary Affairs

by

Thomas G. Evans

Associate Professor of Accounting and International Business
University of South Carolina

This publication is designed to provide accurate and au-
thoritative information in regard to the subject matter
covered. It is sold with the understanding that the pub-
lisher is not engaged in rendering legal, accounting, or
other professional service. If legal advice or other expert assistance is required, the services of a competent
professional person should be sought.

*From a Declaration of Principles jointly adopted by a
Committee of the America Bar Association and a Committee of Publishers.*

Published by Dow Jones Books
P.O. Box 300, Princeton, NJ 08540

Printed and bound in the United States of America
10 9 8 7 6 5 4 3 2 1

Library of Congress Cataloging in Publication Data

Evans, Thomas G.
    The Currency Carousel.

    1. International finance.
    2. Foreign exchange problem.
    I. Title
HG3881.E848   332.4'5   77-2305
ISBN 87128-535-5 pbk.

Contents

3027099

Contents

Contents

CHAPTER V A NEW ERA

INTRODUCTION

In many ways, the 1970s represent a significant change from the 1960s. A modern-day Rip van Winkle, having gone to sleep in the 1960s and awakening in the 1970s, might not believe that only a decade, 10 years, has passed. Many ideas, thought patterns, and commonly accepted ways of doing things prevalent in the 1960s and foreseen as continuing into the 1970s are no longer here. Thus, for some critical areas of life, a comparison of the 1960s and 1970s would give the impression that they are a century apart rather than just a decade.

One such area is international monetary affairs. After more than 25 years with a fixed rate monetary system, the world saw it collapse to be replaced with the opposite kind of system, a floating system that nobody really wanted initially. But despite efforts to return to the monetary methods of the past, we find the floating rate system firmly entrenched with little prospect of change in the near future.

Not only has the structure of the world's monetary system changed dramatically in a short period of time but, concurrently, the significance and importance of monetary affairs have grown phenomenally. In fact, few areas of contemporary life have not been affected by changes in the relative value of currencies. In addition, the general public's interest in and awareness of monetary topics have expanded. The value of the dollar, our trade and payment balances, and monetary negotiations have moved from the back pages of newspapers to the front pages and have become prominent issues.

This situation has created the need for a new

book on the monetary affairs of the 1970s, one that will focus on the causes and consequences of the international monetary crises of the 1970s and on the new era of monetary affairs that has emerged. The need is for a concise, easily understood and practical treatment of the monetary topics of today, especially written for those with little or no formal academic background in monetary affairs.

The Currency Carousel is designed to meet these needs. It is an explanation of the major issues in contemporary monetary affairs written for those with a need to know: businessmen, executives, politicians, and students who are interested in monetary affairs or work in this dynamic area. This book can be used as the text or as a supplement to the text in university courses in international business and in executive development programs. It is definitely not intended to be a technical treatment of monetary affairs for the economic scholar.

The book follows a general chronological sequence in Chapters I and II, starting with the Bretton Woods Agreement of 1944 and tracing monetary affairs to December 1976, with an emphasis on events from 1971 to the end of 1976. Chapter I describes the Bretton Woods Agreement, the problems which arose within it and caused its collapse and the creation and collapse of the Smithsonian Agreement. Chapter II focuses on the floating exchange rate system which emerged in 1973; examines its operation to the end of 1976, with special emphasis on the history of the European Joint Float and the series of international monetary meetings since 1974. A series of papers about the floating rate system, pro and con is presented in Chapter III. Chapter IV deals with the modern history of monetary gold and especially the role of gold in monetary affairs today. Chapter V presents an analysis of these events and some conclusions about this very dynamic period in monetary history.

The style of the book is quite similar to *The Monetary Muddle* (Dow Jones Books, 1974); i.e., it employs the practical business style of *The Wall Street Journal.* Whenever possible, background information is presented to facilitate an understanding of the events being described. Unlike the *Mudle,* the majority of the content of this book is my personal account and views, although heavily influenced by the reports found in the *Journal* and *Barron's.* Correspondingly, responsibility for errors of omission, commission, and poor judgment is mine. Periodically, the opinions of the editors of the *Journal* and *Barron's* and other editorial page writers and reports are included to provide different views and critical commentary on the events being covered.

This book is compatible with the *Muddle.* In a real sense, the *Muddle* concentrated on the emergence of the floating rate system and its early operation. However, *The Currency Carousel* covers a broader period and goes more deeply into the reasons and consequences of the monetary events that occurred. Both books overlap somewhat, but the present text is more comprehensive.

In writing *The Currency Carousel,* special appreciation is due my colleagues at the College of Business Administration at the University of South Carolina, especially Dean Jim Kane and Accounting Program Director Howard Sanders. Sam Lett, now with Auburn University at Montgomery, provided some fine research assistance. Special thanks to Bill Beardsley, Dow Jones Books, for the original suggestion and to Marilyn, Becky, and Jon-Jon for their loving support, encouragement, and sacrifice.

THOMAS G. EVANS, PH.D.
Columbia, S. C.

There is a story often told that says that in the whole world there are just two persons who really understand international monetary affairs—*and they disagree!*

Chapter I

The Fixed Rate Fix

Some Basics

An appropriate issue to consider at the beginning of this book is, "Why do we have an international monetary system?" Consideration of this question leads to even more basic ones: "Why do we have money?" and "Why do we have national states?" The answers go beyond the scope of this book, but if we accept the need for money and the reality of national states, we can examine their relevance to an international monetary system.

The existence of money and national states leads to the establishment of national currencies. Each state will have its own money and quite naturally, a national bias towards that currency will develop. In business and economic activity, the bias for national currency (which is cost-based and thus selling-price reflected) means that for any economic activity that crosses national lines, a mechanism is needed for exchanging national currencies.

If we had no nations, no money, or no bias for national currency, then possibly we would not need international monetary transactions or they could be simplified. While these observations may seem obvious, in reality the bias for national currency and currency nationalism greatly complicates international monetary affairs at every turn and should not be overlooked.

Given money, nations, currency nationalism and international business, some sort of relationship, formal or informal; structured or unstructured, must exist between the national currencies involved. If international trade is significant, the relationship between the currencies will become significant as well. In fact, it is this growth in international trade in recent years that has catapulted monetary affairs into the position of prominence it occupies today.

The Bretton Woods Agreement

Toward the close of World War II, the major Allied leaders exercised considerable foresight in meeting in Bretton Woods, New Hampshire in 1944 to establish a postwar international monetary system. Perhaps realizing the need for a stable structure to facilitate the restoration of an industrial world largely devastated by the war, or perhaps cognizant of the new structure of power among the nations resulting from the war, or perhaps dissatisfied with the previous times of instability and problems with gold-base systems, they forged ahead on a new monetary system, a fixed rate system.

The agreement was signed in 1944 and took effect in 1945. It created an international agency, the International Monetary Fund, with the following major objectives:

(1) To promote international monetary cooperation among the nations;

(2) To help expand and balance the growth of international trade; and

(3) To promote exchange rate stability and maintain monetary arrangements.

The fixed rate system had the following major features: Each member nation of the Fund defined a par value for its own currency in terms of gold or the U.S. dollar; the United States defined the value of the dollar in terms of gold only; each nation agreed to regulate the market exchange rate for its currency within a band of plus or minus 1% of its par value, either by purchasing its own currency in the market to increase its value when it was too low or by selling its currency to reduce the market price when it was too high; and nations could change the par value of their currencies after consultation with the IMF (the change was called a devaluation if the new value was lower; a revaluation if higher).

The IMF also provided temporary financial assistance to member nations experiencing monetary difficulties. Each nation upon joining the IMF was assessed a quota to be paid, one-fourth in gold and three-fourths in its own currency. This pool of gold and national currencies became available to nations when needed for short term balance of payment problems and adjustments.

The Bretton Woods system was similar to previous monetary arrangements, most notably the gold standard and modified gold standard. These systems worked well, but often too well by inflexibly imposing harsh economic adjustments on nations who erred. The new system was in reality a gold-dollar system with flexibility. The dollar was the central currency—it alone was defined in terms of gold and all other currencies were defined in dual terms, dollars and gold. Over time, gold and the dollar became the most popular reserve assets, and eventually dollars which were more plentiful and could earn interest, prevailed over gold as a reserve asset. Thus, nations felt free to accumulate dollars which then became the dominant monetary item of the system. Since the dollar was convertible into gold, it was considered as good as gold. The U.S. with its spending around the world to aid reconstruction, its foreign aid program, and its troops on foreign soil saw to it that plenty of dollars were available.

Malfunctions Develop

(For a time, the Bretton Woods world monetary system worked well. It was designed to give the nations of the world a stable monetary system with flexibility through occasional devaluations and revaluations of par values to handle any imbalances without too much disturbance of the overall stability.) By and large, the postwar period was a time of economic growth, greater prosperity, increasing international trade and currency rate stability. However, some situations related to the operation of this flexible adjustment process began to signal trouble ahead:

(1) The adjustment process depended upon the voluntary action of the nation involved in response to economic realities. However, the political and national implications of those adjustments often made nations reluctant to take the steps clearly called for. For example, a nation with a persistent payments deficit, instead of devaluing its currency, could continually try to prop up the value of its currency and avoid the devaluation as long as possible. Why? Because a devaluation has negative political and psychological implications and economically increases the cost of imports to that nation. In a devaluation, since the new value of the currency is lower, there is a national feeling of shame, economic error and punishment. As a result some nations resisted downward pressure on their currencies and caused the system to overheat.

(2) A special case of the same kind of problem concerned the American dollar. In the latter part of the 1960s, the American trade and payment deficits clearly called for a devaluation of the dollar but in addition to the arguments raised above, the central role of the dollar in the system argued against a dollar devaluation, since the parities of the whole system would

change. Over time, the dollar became overvalued and ripe for crisis.

(3) On the other hand, a special problem also arose for nations with surplus payment balances whose response should have been a voluntary revaluation. But the domestic consequences would have been to curtail exports and to lose business and jobs. Thus, these national governments found it convenient to resist such actions with the result that they accumulated large quantities of foreign currency which eventually were converted into dollars. The ripples of this situation are still with us today.

Eventually monetary crises began to develop in the Bretton Woods system. They concerned the major non-dollar world currencies and gold in the late 1960s and finally, the dollar in the early 1970s. The pound sterling, the second major world currency, underwent a crisis and was devalued in 1967. In 1968, gold was the cause of a crisis. Members of the London gold pool (the United States, United Kingdom, Belgium, Italy, the Netherlands, West Germany, and Switzerland) who had agreed in 1961 to control the price of gold in the London free market gave up in March, 1968, after having used up a great deal of national gold stocks in an attempt to keep the price of gold down. The French franc was devalued in 1969. The West German mark was revalued in 1969.

In an effort to alleviate some of the special problems related to the increasing dominance of dollar-based liquidity, the IMF in 1969 created and issued a special form of paper money, Special Drawing Rights (SDRs), to member nations in order to give them additional reserve assets with the IMF. These SDRs could only be used within the IMF system and were equivalent to lines of credit for nations in times of payment problems. It was hoped this additional international liquidity would give the Bretton Woods system more flexibility in the future.

The dollar's turn arrived in the early 1970s although that crisis had its roots in the 1960s. During that decade, America experienced an ever-growing trade and payments deficit which put downward pressure on the dollar and built up a large supply of dollars in foreign hands which could be eventually turned in for American gold.

In the late 1960s and early 1970s, the U.S. involvement in the Vietnam conflict had a strong impact on the American balance of payments and trade, in addition to its impact on American politics and society. The enormous cost of aid to Vietnam, military programs and grants, and the cost of maintaining American forces in Vietnam and elsewhere accelerated the outflow of dollars and increased the severity of the balance of payment and trade deficits. Domestically, Vietnam spending put additional strains on the American economy and contributed toward the increasing rate of inflation, which further weakened confidence in the soundness of the dollar.

Nations with continual trade and payment surpluses built up reserve assets largely in dollars and thus much of the currency reserves of the world were in dollars. The climate of crisis of the late 1960s soon focused on the dollar and a lack of confidence developed. This could have led to a massive conversion of foreign held dollars into gold and completely drained the stock of American gold. However, it did not happen that way.

The U.S. Backs Out

Instead, by August 1971, it had become clear that the United States faced its first major modern currency crisis. The alternatives open to the U.S. were (a) to negotiate or (b) to take unilateral action. Negotiations with the other major nations of the IMF would have attempted to get changes in the Bretton Woods Agreement to prevent an all-out run on American gold. Unilateral action would have the same basic objective. The U.S. did the latter.

President Nixon announced the United States decision to a very surprised world on Sunday, August 15, 1971. Most Americans were caught up with the domestic aspects of the decision: a 10% surcharge on imports and a 90-day freeze on wages and prices. But the rest of the world focused on the third part of the decision: the suspension of gold convertibility of the American dollar which closed the gold window at the United States. No doubt the nations accumulating dollars over the years in the expectation of turning them in for American gold were caught unawares.

In effect, the U.S. action ended the Bretton Woods Agreement. The immediate reaction of international monetary markets was to stay closed for the next week. When the markets reopened on Monday, August 23, most currencies were afloat against the dollar as financial experts struggled for a negotiated settlement to this major monetary crisis.

In retrospect, we can indentify three basic causes of the monetary crisis which emerged in 1971:

(1) the voluntary adjustment process of the agreement did not work as intended;

(2) the American dollar as the central currency had too much resting on it and could not be easily adjusted to changing monetary and domestic situations;

(3) the dollar had dominated gold as a reserve asset to an unexpected degree.

The dollar crisis was not dealt with early enough to avert a major monetary crisis. There is no way of telling how effective any attempts to change the system in the late 1960s would have been, but we can see now what should have been done at that time.

The Wall Street Journal editorial presented on the following page as Reading 1 appeared on August

19, 1971, and shows the mood of the time and the realization that a new monetary order is due. It also presents a concise survey of the major problems that developed in the Bretton Woods Agreement.

READING 1

A New World Monetary Order

Over the next few weeks, Western nations will be deciding the shape of a new world monetary system. If the new arrangement is to have much chance of success, it will have to include more flexibility than its predecessor.

When the U.S. and other nations planned the old system at Bretton Woods, N. H. in 1944, they did not intend that exchange rates should remain forever fixed. The monetary officials recognized that internal developments in member countries could raise or lower the values of their currencies, so they made provision for regular consultations to determine when or whether various rates should be changed.

The overriding aim of the planners, after all, was to promote the freest possible flow of trade and investment. In a free market, the value of anything, even a nation's currency, always is subject to change.

For several years everything appeared to be working well. World trade expanded enormously, as tariffs and other restrictions were steadily pared away.

To be sure, the U.S. in the early 1950s began suffering regular payments deficits, but most other nations welcomed the outflowing dollars as additions to their currency reserves. More or less accidentally, the world went on a dollar standard.

In the 1960s, however, the monetary order began to crumble. U.S. inflation cut into America's exports. Other nations, recovered from the war, became much more vigorous competitors in markets both inside and outside the U.S. America's surplus of exports over imports, which had limited the outflow of dollars, began dwindling away.

U.S. spending on Europe's defenses, moreover, continued high, and in the mid-1960s the outlay on Vietnam accelerated. Foreigners found that the influx of dollars was inflating their domestic economies and yet, with fixed exchange rates, they were committed to take all the dollars that came their way.

In some nations, such as Britain, domestic inflation stemmed more from domestic policies than from the inflow of dollars. In any case, the dollar, the pound and other currencies came under recurring pressures that, in a free market, would have led to changes in values.

By this time, though, fixed exchange rates had become almost a religion. The U.S. argued, with considerable justification, that the dollar's central position demanded that its value remain unchanged; something had to serve as a benchmark for the system. If there had to be changes in values, in other words, they should come in other currencies.

But other nations also were reluctant to move. When a government devalues the currency it admits the failure of its economic policies. On the other hand, a government that revalues its currency upward makes its exports more expensive, a move that can have highly adverse economic consequences for a nation as export-dependent as West Germany.

So everyone for a long time tried to avoid any such developments. The U.S. defended the dollar by imposing various restrictions on private foreign investment, for instance. Other nations, faced by the prospect of devaluation or revaluation, tried various other curbs on the flow of trade and commerce.

The primary aim of the Bretton Woods planners—commercial freedom—thus suffered because of something the planners never envisaged, a fanatic determination to cling to fixed exchange rates.

Determination, though, was not enough, as those businessmen who must trade in foreign currencies appeared to realize. As pressures mounted to push a currency either up or down, the traders bought or sold to protect themselves—and thus intensified the pressures. Eventually a nation in such a situation was forced either to alter its currency's value officially or to let it float freely in the market as the U.S. has now done with the dollar.

It would have been better if the system had been reshaped through voluntary international action, instead of being compelled by the U.S. move. There was no assurance, however, that other countries were ready to offer such cooperation. The best that can be hoped for is that the U.S. and other nations will now work together toward a new arrangement without the inflexibility that helped doom the old system.

As Commerce Secretary Maurice Stans indicated this week, evolution of a viable new order will permit removal of controls on capital outflows. It also should permit elimination of the new import surcharge, as well as many of the other restrictions imposed not only by the U.S. but other nations.

It should, in sum, permit a long step toward the freedom the planners envisioned in Bretton Woods in 1944.

Reaction and Results—The Float

The world's reaction to the American move was largely negative, as could be expected. Since the U.S. unilaterally broke its agreement with the other IMF nations, this was considered unfair. Those nations with payment surpluses whose inventories of dollars were high were now faced with what to do with the dollars, especially if convertibility into gold was not restored. This problem came to be called the "dollar overhang." Export oriented nations were concerned about the domestic economic impact of the U.S. 10% surcharge and their future ability to export to the U.S. Above all, the world monetary system was unhinged by the American action with no clear picture as to where monetary affairs were headed.

The American action was the more worrisome because there was no contingency plan under the Bretton Woods Agreement or among world monetary officials for this kind of situation. A tremendous change had taken place in a short period of time: on Friday, August 13, the Bretton Woods Agreement had ruled; On Monday, August 16, uncertainty and confusion ruled. An agreement of more than 25 years' standing was unilaterally and surprisingly ended, leaving uncertainty and confusion in its wake.

As an interim measure, currencies were allowed to float when the money markets opened about a week later. In a floating system (or nonsystem as its critics call it), the values of currencies are determined mainly by supply and demand in the market. A float is called "pure" if nations do not interfere with the market and allow supply and demand to determine value; but if national governments *do* interfere by buying or selling currencies through their central banks, the float is called "dirty" or "managed." A critical feature of the dirty or managed float is the absence of any requirement that nations regularly intervene in the market; they are free to intervene when they feel it is appropriate and try not to let private individuals know what intervention plans they have. The float that emerged in August, 1971, was managed. In the absence of any formal arrangements, that's all nations could do until another system came into force.

As monetary officials met to negotiate, the following major proposals were made to replace the float:

(1) Devalue the dollar and return to the gold standard under which each nation would define its currency's value in terms of gold and each currency would be freely convertible into gold.

(2) Revise the Bretton Woods Agreement by (a) an immediate devaluation of the dollar, (b) a corresponding rise in the price of gold and (c) elimination of the special role of the dollar with only gold and SDRs as reserve assets. This position was advocated by the European nations.

(3) Continue the float and have a floating system determine the value of currencies (with or without government "assistance").

An additional issue of great importance was the dollar overhang. Throughout the early days of this crisis, the American position was one of firmly demanding adjustment of other currencies upward to help reverse the American payments deficit.

While currencies floated, the difficult and sensitive monetary negotiations were carried out by the finance ministers from the Group of 10, a group of industrial nations (Belgium, Canada, France, Germany, Italy, Japan, the Netherlands, Sweden, United Kingdom, and the United States) which was formed in 1962. Representatives of these member nations met in London and Washington in September and in Rome at the end of November.

Much of the early negotiations focused on modifying the American and European positions that the other side make all the concessions. The U.S. blamed other over-valued currencies for the dollar's current problems; the Eurpeans blamed the U.S. for the current crisis. During the negotiations, the U.S. had little to lose from standing firm. The dollar daily floated upward. Thus, basically what the Americans wanted was being accomplished while they negotiated. The major issues were finally settled in December at a meeting of President Nixon and French President Pompidou in the Azores. The U.S. agreed to accept a devaluation of the dollar and a general realignment of all other currencies. It was left to the finance ministers of the Group of 10 to work out the details when they met three days later at the Smithsonian Institution in Washington.

The Smithsonian Agreement

The "details" that emerged came to be known as the Smithsonian Agreement, which called for another fixed rate world monetary system. However, there were major differences between it and the Bretton Woods Agreement:

(1) The dollar was devalued approximately 9% and other currencies were set at revalued official rates (for example, increases of 16% for the yen, 13% for the West German mark and 7% for the Italian lira).

(2) The official price of gold was raised from $35 to $38 per ounce.

(3) Member nations agreed to control their currencies within a band of plus or minus 2.25% around the new central values (as contrasted with the 1% band of the Bretton Woods Agreement).

(4) The dollar remained unconvertible into gold.

It was hoped that this new agreement, which was soon ratified by the IMF, would create stability. It had brought the long needed devaluation of the dollar and the equally needed expansion in the bands around the currencies. It represented a historical event in monetary affairs—the first devaluation of the American dollar in 25 years. With the crisis resolved and the dollar lower, it was hoped that American exports would now be less expensive and, in turn, that the American trade balance would improve in the near future. This should then lead to an improvement in the American payments balance, thus resolving the major problem that had developed with the dollar. The increase in the value of other currencies would reinforce this sequence of events.

The Smithsonian Agreement was greeted initially with enthusiasm. It was a negotiated settlement of the biggest monetary crisis of the past quarter century. Moreover, what emerged was remarkably similar to the Bretton Woods Agreement with which everyone was familiar and which had earned a great deal of respect. Both sides in the negotiations had been reconciled and might now return to a period of stability. World leaders tempered their optimism, however, by noting a continued need for long term reform of the monetary system. And nations with a large supply of dollars no doubt remained concerned about the convertibility issue.

Problems Again

As it turned out, 1972 was not to be a year of monetary stability. The problems that had developed in the Bretton Woods Agreement did not evaporate. During 1972, confidence in the dollar, despite the Smithsonian devaluation, continued to decline, aggravated by continued U.S. trade and payment deficits. Although the actual figures for the U.S. trade and payment deficits could provide an objective basis for optimism in the dollar, the doubts of the 1971 crisis persisted and the Smithsonian accord began to flounder. Other nations were pledged to keep the dollar within its new bands and they began to feel strain as they increasingly intervened in world currency markets to buy dollars to prop up its value and to keep the value of their own currencies down. Inflation became a major domestic concern in 1972 in most industrial nations. One of the last things an inflation-conscious government wanted to do was to print "extra" money to finance the acquisition of dollars, because that extra currency would eventually find its way back home and fuel inflation even more. The dollar was still in trouble and was again the focus of monetary concern in 1972.

A critical factor to recognize in analyzing the operation of any fixed rate monetary system is the role of speculation and confidence in a given currency. Although there is no accurate measure of how much speculation occurs, the role of speculators—the gray ghosts of every currency crisis—cannot be ignored. In a fixed rate system, nations are pledged to intervene in monetary markets to keep a currency value within a band. However, if continued pressure is put on that currency, the nation may adjust its central value through a devaluation or revaluation. Thus, currency values can be significantly altered by governmental action at a point in time. Inevitably, there are those who will attempt to anticipate governmental action and to benefit from it. In reality, this is no different from speculation in land or securities, but since it deals with currency, it has acquired a special stigma.

For example, in 1972, some were not convinced that the dollar had been devalued enough or that strong currencies had been revalued enough. They believed that the dollar would have to be devalued again and other currencies would go up in value as well. If a significant number of individuals who hold dollars follow their beliefs by selling dollars and buying preferred currencies, their actions guarantee that their anticipations will occur. The results are akin to a widespread belief that the stock market will decline. If people act on this belief, the market indeed declines as they sell their stock, encouraging others to sell, driving prices even lower.

This is not to say that speculation is eliminated in a floating rate system. But its impact is less because in a pure float, the governments are not committed to any central or par value and the currency will not be devalued or revalued by government action at a given point in time. Thus, currencies will float up or down and speculators are free to bet on their movement either way. But currencies will tend to move more smoothly and less abruptly without the possibility of devaluation and revaluation. In a "managed" or "dirty" float, where governments intervene in currency markets, the governments set internal intervention points and work to keep the value of their currency within those points. Usually these points are informal, secret, and easily changed without anyone knowing it. Thus, government actions are much more difficult to predict and bet against in a dirty float compared with a fixed rate system.

Back to No Agreement

As 1972 drew to a close and monetary troubles continued, it became apparent that the Smithsonian Agreement was not going to work. At the end of 1972 and in early 1973, the dollar again experienced a tremendous loss of confidence, primarily because of U.S. trade deficits and the impact of U.S. inflation. The selling of the dollar was fueled also by speculation that other currencies would soon be revalued again, especially the West German mark. Thus, the days of monetary crisis were once more at hand. The crisis came to a head in February, 1973, when major currency markets in London, Paris, Tokyo, and West Germany closed with the dollar sinking, following meetings among monetary officials of the U.S., France, Japan, West Germany, and the United Kingdom. In the absence of any contingency plan, currencies again floated. The dollar immediately dropped another 10%, the second dollar devaluation in 14 months. On February 12, 1973, the world bid formal farewell to the Smithsonian Agreement and to fixed rate monetary systems, after a reign of 29 years.

Why had the new system failed? Some experts said because it was a fixed rate system and in a day of speculators, powerful multinational corporations, inflationary and anti-inflationary national economic policies a fixed rate system without a great deal of flexibility in central value adjustment just could not work. Others blamed the parameters of the system rather than the system itself, saying that the problems inherited by the Smithsonian Agreement were not adequately resolved by the first devaluation of the dollar and that the dollar should have been devalued more and other currencies revalued more for the sytem to work.

In all fairness to the Bretton Woods Agreement, its degree of success was amazing; imagine any international agreement among the major non-Communist industrial nations lasting as long as it did and working well most of the time.

Whatever the reason, world monetary leaders were not as quick to meet and set up a new fixed rate system to replace the Smithsonian as they had when the Bretton Woods Agreement collapsed. The float was there as an interim measure and it emerged as somewhat of a haven in times of currency crisis. Allowing currencies to float gave time for the crisis to cool off and monetary leaders to consider their next moves. But in reality, in February, 1973, the fixed rate reign was over—for at least for the foreseeable future.

During the period covered by the Bretton Woods and Smithsonian agreements, nothing characterized and dominated monetary thinking more than the assumed relationship between changes in currency values and trade balances. The strong belief in the cause-effect relationship of devaluations leading to improvements in the trade balances became almost sacred and guided much of the monetary strategy of the major nations of the world. However, Arthur B. Laffer, now Professor of Economics at the University of Southern California, challenged this belief in a number of controversial papers, two of which were published in *The Wall Street Journal* and are presented below as Reading 2. Contrary to accepted thought, Laffer argues that devaluation may not play a dominant role in improving trade balances and in fact, may hurt a national economy by fueling domestic inflation. Both articles relate these ideas to the American dollar devaluations of 1971 and 1973.

READING 2

Do Devaluations Help Trade?

ARTHUR B. LAFFER

In policy as well as academic circles, it is widely believed that changes in exchange rates cause changes in trade balance. Devaluations are believed to lead to improved trade balances, while revaluations are supposed to lead to worsened trade balances. Yet, more than a year after the Smithsonian accord, the U.S. trade balance has shown no sign of improving. According to many people, we need just a little more time for the devaluation to have its effects.

While obviously not definitive, the evidence presented here places doubt on the notion that devaluations bring about improvements in trade balances: the trade balance being one of the major components of the balance of payments, that component thought to be most responsive to exchange rate changes. In addition, the evidence points very strongly to a close and lasting relationship between changes in trade balances and changes in relative rates of growth. The theory of this latter relationship being firmly placed on the well-accepted notion that a country's net demand for foreign goods depends upon its level of income.

The popular theory behind the relationship between exchange rates and trade balances is straightforward. A representative statement of that theory as it pertains to the U. S. might proceed as follows: By raising the dollar price of foreign exchange (devaluation of the dollar), the dollar cost of foreign goods will naturally rise. In a like manner—because the foreign exchange price of the dollar has fallen as a consequence of U.S. devaluation—the foreign currency price of American export goods will now be lower. Americans will buy less of the now higher-priced foreign goods, while at the same time, American export goods should sell better abroad because of the decline in the price foreigners have to pay for them. The end result of a dollar devaluation should be an improvement in the overall U.S. trade balance (U.S. exports minus U.S. imports), though perhaps only after a lag of as much as two years.

Nothing appears to be more at odds with this theory than the current trade balance picture of the U.S. In May-June of 1970, the foreign currency value of the U.S. dollar depreciated by about 6%, vis-a-vis the currency of out major trading partner, Canada. A year later, the dollar depreciated again relative to the Swiss franc, the German mark, the Austrian schilling and the Dutch guilder. Between August of 1971 and the beginning of 1972, the dollar was further devalued versus virtually every major currency.

In sum, during 1970, the dollar depreciated (on a trade weight basis) by nearly 3% relative to our principal industrial trading partners. In 1971, there was a further depreciation of about 6% and during the first three quarters of 1972, the foreign currency value of the dollar depreciated an additional 2%.

While the foreign currency value of the dollar was depreciating, the U.S. trade balance, instead of improving as the theory would predict, was actually going further into deficit. Since the middle of 1970, the U.S. merchandise trade balance has continuously deteriorated, moving from an export surplus of about $3 billion annually to the early 1973 deficit rate of about $6 billion—an overall deterioration of some $9 billion annually after two and one-half years of continued depreciation of the dollar. Nor can poor price performance in the U.S. be blamed for this deteriorating trend. Compared to most foreign prices, U.S. prices have performed quite reasonably since mid-1970 as well as over the past decade or so.

Although some argue that the failure of the U.S. to improve its trade balance is due to offsetting special circumstances, it should not come as a total surprise to those who have observed other countries' experiences with devaluations or revaluations. Of the major devaluations since 1950, few have been followed by significant improvements in the particular country's trade balance.

For the devaluation experiences of Britain, Spain, Denmark and Austria, the trade balance was as bad, if not worse, three years after devaluation as it was the year prior to devaluation. Of some 14 convertible currency devaluation experiences that I have examined, a full 10 had larger deficits in trade three years after devaluation than they had in the year immediately preceding the year of devaluation.

The revaluation picture is not very different, but there are very few examples, and German mark revaluations account for nearly all of them. The effective number of revaluations that Germany has carried out depends upon how one treats changes in border tax adjustments. But, irrespective of precisely how many times the German mark has been revalued, it would be no mean task to discern a substantial deterioration in the German trade balance. Thus, given at least a casual look at the historical experience of foreign countries, it should not come as a complete surprise that the U.S. trade balance has not turned around since the foreign currency value of the dollar started to decline.

While trade balances may not respond predictably to exchange rate changes, they do appear to be quite closely related to differential growth rates. When a country increases its economic growth rate relative to its trading partners, we often find a deterioration in that country's trade balance. Perhaps the closest of the relationships is to be found between the U.S. and other industrial countries.

The corresponding relationships for Japan, the European Economic Communities and the United Kingdom are also very close. Other factors, including some associated with the special characteristics of individual countries, explain persistent deficits or surpluses in individual natins. But in each case, an increase in the differential between domestic and foreign growth is usually associated with a deterioration in the trade balance.

In the most recent of times perhaps more policy measures than ever have been pushed through in the hope of improving the U.S. trade position. The dollar has been devalued, capital controls and trade restrictions have continued to sprout everywhere, Export-Import bank outlays have grown, voluntary quotas have been placed on a number of commodities, anti-dumping and contervailing duty measures have been threatened, and so on.

In face of it all, the trade balance has proceeded much as usual.

When we consider how rapidly the U.S. has grown recently, it seems reasonable that the growth rate will taper off in the future. The rest of the world, on the other hand, has recently been growing slowly relative to historical norms and should show some resurgence. If foreign growth does rise and U.S. growth slackens, we should expect a noticeable improvement in the U.S. trade balance. This improvement should, in my opinion, be attributed to U.S. growth relative to foreign growth, and not (as it probably will) to the delayed effects of devaluation.

From a theoretical standpoint, the relationship between a country's trade balance and its relative rate of growth is based entirely upon the well-accepted notion that the higher a country's income is, the more that country will import. Thus, as is well documented in virtually all elementary textbooks, net imports depend upon income. Changes in net imports depend, therefore, on changes in income. And changes in net imports, as a share of GNP, depend upon a country's growth rate.

Any one country's imports are necessarily the exports of the rest of the world, and its exports are the rest of the world's imports. Therefore, a country's trade balance surplus is the rest of the world's deficit. Because one country's trade balance surplus is all other countries' deficit, that country's trade balance must likewise depend upon the growth of the rest of the world, as well as its own growth rate. Therefore, based solely on the notion that the level of a country's imports depends on its income, we find that changes in its trade balance (or current account) should depend upon changes in its growth rate relative to the rest of the world.

From a policy standpoint, there are several observations that can be made concerning the balance of trade. (The reader must again be careful to distinguish between the balance of trade and the overall balance of payments.)

First, while no one can say for sure that exchange rate changes do not matter, it appears fair to say that their effects on the trade balance and thereby domestic employment have been treatly exaggerated in policy discussions.

Second, I think the use of the trade balance as a policy indicator distinct from domestic growth has probably been overdone and should be played down. Thus, much of the blame placed on the current administration for poor trade performance should properly be praise for bringing about rapid economic growth.

Third, both official and private pessimism as to the future American trade position also appear to me to have been substantially overstated. While we may not soon again see the surpluses of the late Forties, the very recent trade deficits also appear to be somewhat abnormal.

Finally, although no one can ever deny with certainty that trade measures other than exchange rate changes help the trade balance, there is a widely held presumption in policy discussions that these trade measures do matter and matter a lot. This point of view has clearly been given too much weight in trade policy. The trade balance, like many other economic indicators, responds both predictably and in a logical way to the overall economic environment. Using gimmicks to alter the trade balance is to a large extent futile, and perhaps even mischievous.

The Bitter Fruits of Devaluation

ARTHUR B. LAFFER

Inflation is plaguing not only the housewife but also the economics profession. Over 1973, wholesale prices rose 18.2% and consumer prices rose at a rate of nearly 9%. Conventional economic views did not predict and cannot explain increases of this magnitude.

The money supply has expanded at a rate some consider too high from a policy perspective, but not one that is terribly high for comparable periods over the past decade. Using past relationships between rates of growth of the money supply and inflation as our guide, it is virtually inconceivable that excessive money growth is to blame for the almost unprecedented rate of inflation recently experienced.

For quite some time now fiscal policy has been if anything contradictory. The full employment budget has been balanced, the actual deficit has shrunk and total outlays have been tightly controlled. Even government purchases, which in real terms soared prior to 1969, have been substantially reduced. All in all fiscal policy does not appear to be the culprit.

Advocates of Phillips curves, price bulges and a whole host of other views are also faced with an inordinate amount of inflation to explain with inadequate sources. Unemployment is higher than at many times in the recent past, yet inflation is higher than at any time. Even the overall price controls program couldn't have increased inflation this much.

Nor can the recent high rates of inflation in the United States be explained as solely a part of an overall world-wide inflation problem caused by shortages of food and other goods. Over the same period that the rate of inflation in U.S. wholesale prices registered 26.5%, we find the German and British rates at 6.2% and 7.3% respectively. World-wide inflation has been great, but other nations did not experience the sudden burst that struck the U.S.

There is one way, however, to explain a large portion of the sudden burst of price increases in the United States. All economists recognize that the devaluation of the dollar, in December 1971 and again in February 1973, has some inflationary impact. If you view the domestic economy as basically a closed system with a few international inputs, as most economists traditionally have, then you will see this effect as slight. But if you conceive of the U.S. as but a part of a relatively unified world market, the inflationary effect of devaluation must be seen as far more dramatic, indeed fully adequate to explain the kind of inflation the U.S. has recently experienced.

The conventional doctrine relating domestic inflation to currency depreciation is in essence straightforward and simple. When a country devalues, say by 10%, it will now cost $110 to buy the same amount of currency that $100 used to buy. The price of imported goods will automatically rise by the amount of devaluation.

To compute the overall inflationary effect of devaluation, therefore, one need only know the amount of the devaluation and the share of the total goods bundle imports compose. Of total demand in the United States, imports comprise roughly 5%; therefore, according to the conventional approach, a 10% devaluation of the U.S. dollar should add only 0.5% to the appropriate price index—a trifling amount.

While many versions of the conventional view of the inflationary consequences of a devaluation are far more complicated, the above description captures its essence. It is important to note that this view assumes that the foreign currency price of imported goods does not change—only the domestic currency price changes. The prices of all domestically produced goods are also assumed to remain unchanged.

This conventional approach, however, is not the only view of the consequences of devaluation. The chief alternative sees the world economy not as a collection of loosely related closed systems, but as one relatively efficient market. In an efficient market, the price of goods does not depend on the amount flowing from one geographical sector to another.

To determine, say, how a change in the price of apples in Illinois would affect the price of apples in Kansas, very few economists would study the flow of apples from one state to another. Rather, they would expect that even if the traditional flow of apples was little changed, the price in Kansas would rise to compensate for the higher price in Illinois.

Devaluation is an attempt to change the price of apples and other goods in one nation relative to another, by changing the relationship between the yardsticks by which those prices happen to be measured. If markets are efficient, the real price of apples—relative to cars or hours of labor or other things of value—will not be affected. Nor will this real price be different, other things being equal, in one nation or another. Thus, if the yardsticks change, the prices measured by them will have to change in a way that preserves the original relationship of real prices.

Or consider the same phenomenon from the point of view of one nation. If any country produces goods that it both trades and consumes domestically, then items sold for domestic consumption will not differ in price from items sold for foreign consumption. Likewise, foreign imports into any country should also sell at the same price as domestically produced import substitutes—both before and following devaluation. If these prices did not adjust in this manner, speculators could make virtually unlimited profits by purchasing goods in one country and selling them in another country.

Various artificial as well as natural barriers, of course, keep any market from being completely efficient, and these may be higher in international markets than in domestic ones of similar size. But if there ever were any reasons to conceive of international markets as greatly different from domestic ones, they surely have been greatly eroded by the negotiated reduction in trade barriers and improvements in international transportation and communication. The empirical results of devaluations around the world, moreover, are fully consistent with efficiency in international markets.

This alternative view of devaluation predicts, for example, that devaluations do not improve a country's trade balance. Because nominal prices will adjust and real prices will remain unchanged, the devaluing nation will not gain a competitive advantage.

With the available data on the effect of devaluations, in fact, one would be hard pressed to find much of a relationship at all between exchange rate changes and trade balances. This, of course, does not mean that I have proven that a relationship does not exist, only that I have been unable to find one. However, I did find that trade balances appear to be closely related to a country's growth rate relative to other countries. That is, when a country's growth rate increases, its trade balance tends to deteriorate, and contrariwise. This view is entirely consistent with the recent improvement in the U.S. trade balance, coming as it did with the peaking of the U.S. growth rate in 1973.

Similarly, the alternative view predicts that a devaluing nation will suffer rapid inflation relative to the rest of the world. Its nominal price levels will have to increase rapidly to restore the original relationship of real prices with real prices elsewhere in the world. This effect, of course, does not depend on the actual flow of goods from one nation to another. This prediction is also consistent with the U.S. experience with devaluation in the past 30 months or so. Other countries also provide a rich inventory of case studies.

After France's 1958 devaluation, its wholesale price index rose almost 14.5% over the three succeeding years as compared to a rise of 2.4% in Germany, 5% in the United Kingdom, and a fall of 0.1% in the United States. After its 1969 devaluation, France's wholesale price index rose 17% in three years, again more than the contemporaneous U.S., German or British rises. In the three years prior to its devaluation, France had experienced only a 5% increase in its wholesale price index.

Looking at the United Kingdom experience of 1967, a similar pattern emerges. In the three years before the pound was devalued, Britain's wholesale price rise was 6.2%, while in three years after devaluation, the same index rose 16.8%. Equivalent U.S. and German price increases were 9.7% and 4.5%. The relative smallness of the German figure is not surprising when one realizes that the German mark was revalued during the 1968-69 period.

One could go and list experience after experience. One can also from the more limited data notice the precise opposite price effects when a country revalues. While the price effects of exchange rate changes are more distinct using wholesale prices, they are still quite evident using the less volatile consumer prices. Even over long periods of time, the relationship between exchange rate changes and relative rates of inflation remains remarkably close.

On the basis of historical experience in numerous countries, one surely cannot disregard the alternative view of the inflationary consequences of devaluation. In point of fact, it can hardly be coincidental that so much inflation follows directly on the heels of a devaluation in such a large number of episodes. While obviously much more could be done to verify as well as quantify the relationship, both theory and available empirical data suggest that a devaluation has far more than the trifling inflationary impact which the traditional doctrine suggests.

In sum, I personally feel that the mystery of the current bout of inflation in the United States is readily solvable; it is as much a direct consequence of the dollar's devaluations as any other cause. I would hope that our recent experience with devaluations would make policy officials as well as academics slightly more cautious about panaceas. Looking at the current U.S. experience alone, it would seem that a robust turnaround in the trade balance did not come until the rate of economic growth slowed, but that robust inflation took off as soon as devaluation took place.

Chapter II

The Floating Rate Fix

The New Era: Floating

In February, 1973, world monetary leaders once again faced a crisis in world currency markets. It was part of a continuing series of crises that began in 1967 and caused the collapse of two world monetary accords, the Bretton Woods Agreement in 1971 and the Smithsonian Agreement in 1973. The February, 1973 crisis concerned the American dollar, as had the one in August, 1971. The immediate outcome was to let currencies float and the dollar to be devalued by 10% when currency markets opened later in February.

Since this was the second major crisis in a short time, few monetary officials were optimistic about a quick settlement. Although there was turmoil in monetary circles, the devalued dollar promised future trading advantages to the U.S. The amounts recently spent by foreign central banks to support the dollar toward the collapse of the Smithsonian Agreement had found their way to the U.S. instead of being converted into American gold. The repatriated dollars were invested in American securities. This helped finance the U.S. national government and reduce short term interest rates. All in all America's situation was not too bad. But there were problems in other areas. As the dollar dropped and other currencies rose, foreign governments and businesses worried about repercussions on their trade. Monetary leaders feared that each nation would forget years of effort toward international monetary accord and cooperation and take unilateral action to control currency with the aim of achieving unfair trade advantages rather than continuing the degree of free trade achieved.

Meanwhile, currencies floated along, their new values primarily determined by supply and demand, with occasional "assistance" from central banks. In this and the prior currency crisis, the float was there to take over from the fixed rate system when that system collapsed. Even under the Bretton Woods and Smithsonian agreements, some national currencies were allowed to float, usually in time of trouble for that currency; for example, both Canada and Great Britain had allowed their currencies to float in recent times. But these were isolated instances and all other major currencies were fixed. The float has always been a haven in time of storm. Because of that, it has acquired the stigma of being a second best system, i.e., to be used only in times of crisis and then abandoned as soon as a better system, fixed rate, was available. What most concerned monetary leaders about the float was the lack of any central value for their currencies and the difficulties imposed in the long run on trade.

In a long term international business deal, commitments must be made for five, 10, or 20 years in the future. Under a fixed rate system, there are commitments that currencies will have certain values and relationships and that in the absence of special circumstances, these values and relationships will continue. In a float, however, there is no way of knowing where currency values will be next year. This makes long term international planning and financing a problem.

On the positive side, in recent times, floating has proven to be operational compared with the fixed rate system during crisis periods. In actual fact, some advocate the float because of the absence of promises that aren't fulfilled. A case in point involves the claim that under a fixed rate system, long term trade deals are facilitated. Some would point to the recent experience of a number of U.S. and foreign firms who relied upon the Bretton Woods and Smithsonian agreements' fixed rates in long term borrowing decisions and ended up having to pay under the floating currency values. If some nations harbor grudges against the suspension of the Bretton Woods promise of dollar convertibility, then their counterparts are business firms which harbor grudges because they relied upon values that were fixed but now are not longer in effect.

Back in the late 1960s, a number of large international firms, American and foreign, went to the Eurobond and Eurocurrency markets for international financing. These markets were in a stage of growth and rapid expansion and thus able to finance huge loans when such funds were not available elsewhere. The Eurocurrency market was created by national currencies kept on deposit outside natonal boundaries and available from banks free from governmental control and regulation. Eurobonds represent long term loans available in a number of currencies. If an American firm needed long term capital in 1969 to finance an expansion of its European operations, it could go to the Eurobond market to get a loan denominated in any major European currency. For example, assume that an American firm made a decision to borrow 40,000,000 West German marks in June, 1969, to be repaid in 1979. At that time, the DM equaled $.2500 and the dollar cost of repaying the loan in 1979 was expected to be $10,000,000 (ignoring interest). This figure would certainly be critical in evaluating financing alternatives and deciding where to borrow the needed capital. But by June, 1972, just three years later, the central rate used in making that decision no longer applied because of the collapse of the Bretton Woods Agreement and the first devaluation of the dollar. Now the mark had risen in value to $.3150 and the dollar cost of settling the loan had increased to

$12,600,000, an increase of 26% By June, 1973, given the collapse of the Smithsonian Agreement and the second devaluation of the dollar, the mark had risen again, this time to $.3745 and the dollar cost of the loan went up to $14,980,000. Even with these crises over and a degree of calm settling into the currency markets by June, 1976, the mark was still climbing against the dollar and the dollar cost of the loan went to $15,436,000, an increase of over 54%! The two dollar devaluations thus created some real financial concern in American firms with long term debt denominated in revalued currencies. The consequence was to increase the dollar cost of repaying the loans and even to reduce current profits from a financial accounting viewpoint.

Few realized in February, 1973, that the "temporary" float was here to stay, and that a new era had arrived. However, as 1973 continued, there was considerable concern about the lack of progress toward a new international agreement. In March, representatives of the Group of 10, other Common Market nations, the IMF, the Organization for Economic Cooperation and Development, and the Bank for International Settlements met in Paris. But there was little agreement about what to do. At a preparatory meeting in Brussels, the Common Market nations could not even agree on a common stand to bring to Paris and they decided to go back to Brussels for additional meetings. Major currency markets were technically closed at the time of the meeting but currency was actually being traded without central bank intervention. Things looked bad because of the extent of disagreement among the leaders. Special concerns arose about the potential splintering of the monetary world into regional blocs related to major currencies with others, not in any bloc, left on the outside. Some foresaw the development of a dollar bloc, a Japanese bloc, and a European currency bloc.

The Joint European Float

Some believed that the formation of currency-tied blocs was the optimal structure for the world at this time rather than returning to a fixed rate system tied to a single central currency or to gold, or of sticking with a floating system in which currency values are not tied to anything. Advocacy of currency-tied blocs continues today, so the record of the only major currency bloc to develop recently needs closer examination in order to see how well it has worked.

Creation

A joint European float was established in May, 1972, by an agreement among the orignal Common Market nations (France, West Germany, Italy, the Netherlands, Belgium, and Luxembourg), plus the United Kingdom and Denmark. These eight nations agreed to permit their currencies to fluctuate within a narrow band (one-half the general IMF agreement, $1\frac{1}{8}\%$ either way) among themselves, but as a whole to fluctuate within the bands set up by the Smithsonian Agreement (2.25%) against other currencies. This EEC narrow band was called the "snake," due to the linking of the eight currencies. The wider band within which the snake could fluctuate against all other currencies became known as the "tunnel." The snake members agreed to work together to maintain the closer currency values relative to each other and to keep the whole joint float within the wider bands against other currencies, especially the dollar. Since the Common Market nations were committed to an extensive trade among themselves, the joint float prevented a large change in value for any currency which would have a great impact on the trade relations and possibly upset the Common Market. These nations also had a common interest in protecting their currency values against other nations and the joint float was a means to accomplish that. It also introduced a degree of stability into the monetary relationships within the Market and thus fostered trade. The snake was designed to allow some flexibility but to limit excessive movement of the currencies involved. It was a sort of "mini-Smithsonian" fixed rate system within the Smithsonian and represented an emphasis on regional monetary union and cooperation.

This initial union did not last long. Both of the non-EEC nations, the United Kingdom and Denmark, withdrew from the joint float later in 1972, leaving only the Common Market nations in the snake. After the failure of the Paris meeting in March, 1973 to make progress on monetary reform, representatives of the Common Market, which now included the United Kingdom, Ireland, and Denmark in addition to the original six (France, West Germany, Belgium, the Netherlands, Luxembourg, and Italy) went back to Brussels to confer. From that meeting came word that the snake would continue, although now as a floating bloc with no tunnel. That is, six nations (all but the United Kingdom, Ireland, and Italy) agreed to peg their currencies to each other and keep their values within plus or minus 2.25% of the official values. The whole bloc would float against other currencies (called a partial joint float). The West German mark was immediately revalued 3%. A primary purpose of continuing the snake was to prevent the dollar from dropping too much against the European currencies and thus giving the U.S. great trade advantages. The other three Common Market nations decided to continue to float outside the snake.

Throughout 1973, a year of monetary turmoil and uncertainty, the joint float continued. However, it was shocked by a French move in January, 1974. The franc was one of the weaker currencies in the float and France decided to withdraw from the snake and let its commercial franc float alone for a time (originally expected to be six months or so) to establish a more realistic value. It was believed that France did this to help balance its trade accounts. It was expected that the franc would fall in value, and thus make French goods more competitive in world markets and make imports into France more expensive. France was a nation with a dual currency system: the franc used by tourists and others had been floating but francs used in commerce and trade had been linked in the snake. Now France removed official support from the commercial franc and let it float too. The other members of the joint float were upset by the French move but could do nothing. The franc stayed out of the float for 18 months before rejoining in July, 1975.

Controversy

The next event of major importance in the history of the snake came in the fall of 1975 and involved the admission of Switzerland into the joint float. The Swiss sought to join the snake which by then linked the currencies of West Germany, France, Belgium, the Netherlands, Luxembourg, Denmark, and Norway. After many months of discussion, which began in March, 1975, Switzerland received agreement in principle from the other Common Market nations in September. Still to be decided was the official value for the Swiss franc, one of the world's strongest currencies. The Swiss obviously wanted a low value to boost exports and hoped the link would stop its franc from rising too much against the currencies of Switzerland's major trading partners who also happened to be in the snake. The current members of the snake preferred a high value for the Swiss franc to boost their exports to Switzerland, but not so high as to boost the value of the snake and thereby harm trade with other parts of the world. An additional matter was raised about Swiss admission, seemingly unconnected with the value of the Swiss franc. France insisted that as a condition to join the joint float, Switzerland must ease its banking secrecy laws so that citizens of other Common Market nations who were using Swiss banks to evade taxes would be caught. This issue had long bothered European tax collectors and France saw this as an opportunity to get the issue resolved. However, the Swiss resisted, got support from other Common Market nations and won out over the French. France then raised additional conditions related to Swiss control over capital flows and the discussions started anew. In reality, the French were worried that the admission of the highly valued Swiss franc to the snake would increase the value of the French franc and thus hurt exports. The Swiss finally gave up in November and ended their bid to join the snake. Although this marked a stormy period for the snake, additional problems were just around the corner.

Faced with massive domestic and then international economic crises late in 1975, Italy decided to stop supporting the lira in January, 1976. This caused repercussions within the snake. Funds moved quickly out of the lira and the French franc and into the strongest snake currency, the West German mark. Given the agreement to keep currencies aligned, European central banks had to intervene massively to keep the relationships in force. The snake was experiencing the same

.type of problems that the world went through toward the collapse of the Bretton Woods and Smithsonian agreements. For a short time, central bank intervention and statements of determination from European monetary leaders calmed the crisis. But a shattering blow to the snake came in March as the French again decided to withdraw from the monetary union after the lira turmoil put downward pressure on their currency. The French cited two reasons for allowing the franc to float free of the joint float: (1) reluctance of other snake members to make changes in the float arrangement to permit wider band widths and (2) concern about the recent decline in the British pound which the British appeared to have engineered to gain trade advantages.

Collapse?

The immediate impact of the French move was disastrous. Many called this the end of the snake, although France could rejoin at any time. They saw it as foreshadowing an end to monetary and economic cooperation in Europe. On monetary markets, the franc dropped in value and the Danish krone and Belgian franc in the snake came under great downward pressure. Some monetary leaders in the joint float expressed confidence that the snake would continue, and that with some changes the French would rejoin it for a third time, allowing regional monetary cooperation to continue. But in general, the French move was widely interpreted as a major setback for regional monetary cooperation. In the opinion of one monetary banker, the European snake had collapsed and was now only a "worm."

France's exit left the snake with seven members: West Germany, Holland, Belgium, Luxembourg and Denmark as full members, and Norway and Sweden as associate members. The West German mark was clearly the strongest currency in the snake and this continually prompted rumors that it would be revalued. This resulted, periodically, in heavy buying of the mark which put strains on the snake members who had to maintain the currency values within the plus or minus 2.25% band. Had the Swiss been admitted into the snake, the strength of the Swiss franc might have relieved some of the speculative pressure on the mark. Ironically, it was the French who blocked the Swiss from joining the snake, then themselves withdrew.

Other than the "ins and outs" of the French franc, the most significant change in the snake after November, 1973, came in October, 1976 when the West German mark was revalued and realigned against the other snake currencies. This was a part of the monetary crises which followed the Manila IMF meeting and is covered in detail in the section entitled, "Manila Postlude."

The Dirty Float:
Initial Experience

In the aftermath of the Paris talks of March, 1973, currency markets reopened with all major currencies afloat. There was little prospect that a new system of fixed rates would be adopted. Instead, nations adjusted their monetary thinking to setting intervention limits on the floating of their currencies in order to keep their values within "reasonable and realistic" limits. Actually, in the initial months after the Paris meeting, the floating markets were relatively tranquil and a degree of monetary stability returned. After the devaluation of the dollar by 10%, the revaluation of the West German mark by 3% and the establishment of the joint European float, currency values were quite stable. It was a period with bright and dark spots: on the one hand, American trade figures for December, 1972 and January, 1973, showed an improved upward trend; but concerns about the effect of floating on long-run trade, the amount of dollar overhang, and the uncertainties of the future lingered on.

By June, top bankers and monetary officials at the Paris meeting of the American Banking Association had reached a consensus that the float thus far was serviceable and had proven manageable. Part of the adjustment in doing international business involved additional costs in the form of expensive hedging and forward contracts to protect against the uncertainties of future currency movements. Their comments were not inconsistent with previous opinions, since the major concerns about floating mainly refer to the long run rather than its short run impact on trade and investment. One month later, the central bankers of the world met in Basel, Switzrland and their actions (or, lack of action) and public statements were in agreement with the conclusions drawn at the June conference of the ABA. Despite uncertainty and fears about the future, the dirty float was working, and not many were advocating abandoning it and rushing into another sytem. The recent experience with the Smithsonian Agreement was still in monetary leaders' minds and they proceeded with caution. As 1973 continued, the float proved crisis-free and won acceptance.

At this time, another development, somewhat amazing, took place to further stabilize monetary markets. The "trouble-causing" currency that had been responsible for the most recent series of monetary turmoil was behaving and actually rising in value. By late summer, 1973, the American dollar was making a comeback. Although no longer the official central currency in the world system, the dollar was still the world's major currency and reserve asset and its slowly increasing value produced a feeling of confidence in the crisis-weary markets.

There was some disagreement as to the underlying reasons for the dollar's rise: (1) some believed that the dollar had been devalued too much in February and now was rising to a more realistic value; (2) others saw the increase in American interest rates attracting foreign capital to U.S. securities, thus increasing the demand for dollars; and (3) still others felt optimistic about the trend of American trade and payments balances in the near future, based on growing exports of American products, especially agricultural products and capital goods which had become more competitive in price. The increase in the dollar's value, in itself, produced monetary confidence and stability.

Dashed Hopes:
International Meetings

The feelings of satisfaction with the float were not of course, universal. In addition, they must be interpreted in light of concurrent events. All this time, high-level efforts were underway to develop a new system. Expectations were that this process would be complete by September. Thus, expressions of calm and confidence were supported by an assumption that the floating was temporary in order to work out some of the inequalities and problems in world currency relationships, but that monetary reform would be forthcoming.

Those charged with the preparation of a reform proposal were called the Committee of 20, a special committee created by the IMF in 1971. This committee, representing the 120 member nations of the IMF, consisted of six members from major industrial nations (the U.S., United Kingdom, West Germany, France, Japan, and India) and 14 members who represented other IMF nations. Switzerland, who was not an IMF member, had a visitor present at all sessions.

It is interesting to reflect on the status of the IMF at this time. With the collapse of the Smithsonian Agreement and the floating of rates, the IMF had no world monetary system to coordinate and administer and its role had been greatly diminished. But as the only world monetary organization, it continued to be a focal point for monetary discussions and negotiations. No doubt IMF officials expected a fixed rate system to be adopted, shortly putting them back in business. In the meantime, the IMF had no world monetary system to administer.

The Nairobi Agreement

As September drew near, it became apparent that the Committee of 20 would not be ready to present a new proposal to the annual meeting of the IMF at Nairobi, Kenya, and that hopes of ending the floating would be disappointed. In addition, a certain amount of pride would be lost, since Kenya and other Third World nations hoped that a new world monetary agreement would be adopted and that it would be called the "Nairobi Agreement." This would symbolically indicate a new era in monetary affairs in which nations other than the major industrial nations, the U.S., United Kingdom, France, West Germany, and Japan, were important.

The only agreement at Nairobi was to continue the status quo, but as we shall see it gained historical importance for other reasons.

An article by James P. Gannon who attended the Nairobi IMF meeting is presented on the following page as Reading 3. It describes the somewhat awkward position of the IMF going into Nairobi and some of the major issues in the monetary negotiations thus far. It especially focuses on some critical political issues within the IMF itself.

READING 3

Monetary Muddle

JAMES P. GANNON

Imagine the United Nations facing this situation:

All nations are ignoring the basic rules of the UN charter as archaic tenets of a bygone era. The UN's chief executive has been forced to resign, and his replacement, recruited after a long and embarrassing search, is a little-known professor. UN officials suspect the U.S. is trying to undermine the organization's strength. In all, the future of the UN as an effective tool of international cooperation is very much in doubt.

Fortunately, the UN isn't in such a mess. But the "United Nations" of the world of money is. As officials from 126 member countries gather in Nairobi, Kenya, for the September 1973 annual meeting of the International Monetary Fund, the 29-year-old guardian of world currency values finds itself in an awkward position: custodian of a collapsed monetary order, spectator at a new rule-free currency game beyond its control and expectant godfather to a new monetary system not yet born.

"We are living in a period of trouble and transition," concedes a top official of the IMF.

The trouble, of course, is that the old international monetary system, born with the IMF at a 1944 conference at Bretton Woods, N.H., collapsed in stages between August 1971 and March 1973 under the pressure of massive outflows of dollars from the U.S. and orgies of speculation on world currency markets.

The transition from the old Bretton Woods system of fixed currency values currently features an interim arrangement of "floating" exchange rates determined largely by market forces—a situation that mocks all the IMF rules requiring governments to maintain firmly set currency values. The key question is where this transition will lead: negotiations to restructure the monetary system have been under way for nearly a year, but the outline of the new order and the IMF's future role are far from determined.

At the 1973 meeting, further discussions in Nairobi probably will clarify the main outlines of a new monetary system, but authorities agree that a detailed plan won't be ready for IMF approval before the 1974 meeting.

The specific monetary issues are deeply complex and shrouded in the jargon of the specialists. Basically, the negotiators are trying to construct a new system that would require each nation to keep its international inflow and outflow of money in reasonable balance, that would permit changes in any nation's currency value to be made without triggering a crisis and that would generally promote the free flow of investment, trade and development aid among nations.

But those easily stated goals can be reached only through marvelously complex means, and that's what the negotiations are all about. Whatever the final form of the monetary agreement, its ultimate success will depend on how well the IMF, as the policeman enforcing the new monetary rules, can make it work.

The survival of the Washington-based organization as an international lender to financially distressed nations and a center for international monetary deliberations isn't in doubt. But the IMF's future authority, structure and ultimate influence may strengthen or weaken with the changes in the monetary rules.

Some IMF officials fear the overhaul of the currency rules, if lacking enough enforcement authority, could fatally weaken the fund. "The danger of throwing the baby out with the bath water is very considerable," one official says.

And Pierre-Paul Schweitzer, the Frenchman who in August 1973 gave up the IMF helm after 10 years as its managing director, warned that any protracted "delay in restoring an agreed system could erode the legal and moral power" of the IMF. The breakdown of the Bretton Woods monetary system has already "diminished the influence" of the fund, he added.

The way Mr. Schweitzer lost his job and the difficulty the IMF had in recruiting a replacement also have hurt the organization, insiders contend. In effect, Mr. Schweitzer was "blackballed" by U.S. officials, who declined to support him for a third five-year term; the IMF chief ruffled former Treasury Secretary John Connally's feathers by calling for devaluation of the dollar before the Nixon administration was ready to admit that was necessary.

For months, names of "probable successors" and "leading candidates" for the IMF job floated and sank like the dollar. Among a dozen or more such candidates, at least one or two rejected the job, apparently on grounds that the future of the IMF was uncertain and the attitude of the U.S. unfriendly. On July 31, in an appointement that produced a kind of

"Spiro who?" reaction, the IMF finally named its man; H. Johannes Witteveen, a Rotterdam economics professor and former finance minister of the Netherlands.

On appearance, the 52-year-old Mr. Witteveen hardly seems a "take-charge" leader. He is a slight, almost frail-looking man with gray hair and long expressive fingers that sculpt the air as he speaks in a quiet monotone. He presents a gentle, rather stoic image, which may reflect inner qualities of scholarliness and mysticism; he is vice president of an international religious and philosophical movement that seeks to reconcile differences between Christianity and oriental religions.

But associates say his meek appearance may be deceptive. As a former politician and Dutch cabinet member, "he knows what it is to fight battles," says one. "He brings us a nice combination of academics and politics."

While his views on specific monetary issues aren't known, indications are that his general approach will be to stress compromise and accommodation. He's also expected to woo Communist nonmember nations, including the Soviet Union, gradually into the IMF fold.

The new fund chief, a top American official notes, is taking over at the most difficult possible time—when the shape of the future monetary system and the IMF"s role in it are still uncertain. "It would be much easier to come in a year from now," after these questions are settled, he says.

IMF officials argue that the monetary overhaul won't succeed unless member nations are willing to give the fund sufficient authority to make all countries observe rules. "If the fund isn't going to be strong in the future," says one top official, "then in my opinion the reform will have failed."

But most nations, jealous of their sovereignty, don't want the IMF in a position to boss them around. The U.S. is especially leery of granting it much discretionary authority. American officials argue for strong, clear-cut monetary rules but against giving the IMF broad leeway in interpreting them.

The U.S. is wary of too much power at the IMF now that it doesn't run the organization as it once did. In the fund's early years, when the dollar was the world's strongest currency and the American economy stood as a giant among war-battered midgets, the IMF danced to the U.S. tune.

But during the past decade, as the dollar weakened, the U.S. economy was wracked by inflation and as Germany and Japan became financial powerhouses, the IMF has moved out of the shadow of the U.S. Treasury. And as IMF membership grew from its original 45 nations to the present 126, the American voting power was diluted from an initial 38% of the total votes to about 21%. Thus, the U.S. can no longer be sure of having its way.

American officials don't want the IMF telling the U.S. government when it should devalue the dollar or take new steps to fight inflation. A too-strong IMF, it's feared, could create severe political troubles for an administration by pressuring it to take unpopular steps.

"There's an argument that says that these monetary problems are so complex and vary so much from country to country that you have to

turn it all over to an IMF board to exercise
discretionary authority, and the IMF board will
decide when a country has to do something,"
notes Paul A. Volcker, Under Secretary of the
Treasury for Monetary Affairs.

"My own view," he adds, "is that if you
lean too far in that direction, you are putting an impossible burden on the IMF as an
institution, because you are giving it too
much discretionary authority in highly
charged political issues."

This isn't just an American view, Mr. Volcker contends. "A lot of small countries are
just as concerned as we are about giving the
IMF too much discretionary authority."

Some IMF officials view the U.S. stance,
following the "ouster" of the strong-willed
Mr. Schweitzer as evidence that the Americans
are out to weaken the organization. "The
U.S. wants to leave the least amount of discretionary authority with the fund, but you
can't have a strong fund without it," one
official argues.

This question is likely to be settled partly
in the writing of the new monetary rules and
partly in a change in the structure of the fund
itself. There's strong sentiment, backed by the
U.S. and other major nations, to create a new
decision-making body within the fund, made up
of top-level political officials of member governments rather than of financial experts.

"Some high-level policy board will be set
up," predicts an IMF official. Insiders figure
that the new body, probably composed of cabi-
net-level ministers of key governments, would
meet only occasionally to settle the most important issues; more routine matters would be

left to the present executive board, which would be somewhat overshadowed.

Whether the new body would also overshadow the managing director and diminish Mr. Witteveen's authority isn't certain. It's understood he favors the idea but recognizes there's some danger of undercutting his own position.

The main issues in the international monetary negotiations are so complex they've kept the world's experts struggling for a year to find solutions. Here is a brief rundown:

THE ADJUSTMENT PROCESS: Monetary authorities are seeking ways to require nations that run big deficits or surpluses in their international payments to adjust their policies so as to balance their inflow and outflow of funds better. But there's a dispute over whether certain statistical warning signals should almost automatically trigger such corrective actions as a devaluation, as the U.S. wants, or merely call for "consultations" with the IMF, as some Europeans prefer.

EXCHANGE RATES: Fixed currency rates made the old monetary system subject to crisis, but "floating" rates make long-range financial planning difficult. Monetary authorities have agreed to return to "stable but adjustable" par values—a generality not yet backed by a specific scheme. A system of rates somewhat more flexible than the old fixed-rate arrangement is expected.

CONVERTIBILITY: Since Aug. 15, 1971, the U.S. hasn't been willing to exchange gold for dollars. Foreign nations holding billions of dollars want an early return to some form of convertibility. The U.S. agrees that eventually all currencies should be convertible into some kind of monetary assets (not necessarily gold) but isn't ready to assume this obligation for the dollar until the U.S. balande-of-payments situation improves and a new monetary system is put in place.

GOLD AND "PAPER GOLD": Most nations agree that gold should somehow be phased out of the monetary system, because it's a too-scarce, volatile commodity. In its place, the IMF's special drawing rights (SDRs), sometimes called "paper gold," would become the chief reserve asset. But negotiators haven't figured out how to accomplish this transition.

THE "LINK": Poor nations want to link future distribution of SDRs by the IMF to development aid, so that less-developed nations would get a more generous share of the SDRs. While some Europeans are sympathetic, the U.S. fears such a plan would undermine confidence in the SDR.

The Nairobi IMF meeting had to settle for a discussion of the major outlines of a future monetary system rather than the details of such a system. One area of major disagreement concerned the critical adjustment process, previously shown to be a basic cause of the collapse of the Bretton Woods Agreement. The Americans, early in 1973, came out with a new proposal which did not receive a warm reception from other monetary leaders, especially Europeans. Reflecting their position that much of the world monetary crisis and dollar crisis of the 1970s was caused by the failure of other nations voluntarily to revalue and devalue their currencies when appropriate, the American plan called for certain statistical "objective indicators" to be defined, adopted and measured for each nation, such as the level of foreign currency reserves. If an indicator "turned on" for a given nation, it should revalue or devalue its currency. Thus, the authority to instruct a nation would be in the hands of an objective system, and many would know when a nation was acting contrary to the rules. Europeans preferred that such moves be left to the voluntary action of governments. They had some real qualms about the operation of the system: it was vulnerable to "outside influences" (speculators, other governments' intervention) that could set off the indicators and force a nation to change the value of its currency. In addition, the system requires accurate statistics about the nations involved and this was seen as a problem. For these reasons the Europeans were not too receptive to the American proposal.

Other discussions concerned the role of the SDR in future monetary affairs. The SDR (often called "paper gold") was created in 1969 in order to provide an additional form of international reserve asset. Now it was being considered as a solution to one of the most important, long-standing, and sensitive issues in monetary affairs: the dollar overhang, caused by the suspended convertibility of the U.S. dollar. Since 1971, dollars had not been convertible into gold and many nations were caught by the unexpected American move with large inventories of dollars to convert. A way out was offered by the proposal that these dollars be converted into SDRs, which then could be used to increase a nation's reserves, exchanged for other currencies to be used for intervention in the floating currency markets or for international trade and payments. Since the Americans were firm on "no more gold for dollars'', the use of SDRs appeared to be a workable solution to this important issue and worthy of serious consideration.

The SDR offered two potential advantages over gold as a reserve asset: the IMF could control the supply of SDRs available, whereas the amount of gold depended on the limited supply in nature; the SDR's value was potentially more stable, being pegged to the value of the American dollar at this time.

In addition, the SDR was seen as playing another major role: as a form of foreign aid to the less developed nations. When SDRs were created by the IMF they were distributed to all IMF member nations in relation to their original IMF quota contribution. Why not create additional SDRs and distribute them to the underdeveloped Third World nations as a form of aid? This would not decrease the wealth of other nations and thus all would be better off. Moreover, since this aid would come from the IMF, it would carry no additional ''strings'' as direct aid from major nations often does.

The foregoing were the main arguments presented at Nairobi in the issue known as ''the link.'' Third World nations, with little international monetary power and a limited vote in the IMF in the past, suddenly found themselves in a critical political position since their votes were needed to adopt any new monetary system.

Historically, the failure of the IMF to achieve a ''Nairobi Agreement'' on an international monetary system has been more than balanced by the discovery of Third World nations that they had power. Since then, these nations have demonstrated how effective their voices and votes can be, politically and economically, especially when they act as a bloc.

Reading 3 pointed out some of the internal political problems in the IMF itself. As an international agency created and supported by the cooperation and consensus of its member nations, it was subject to political maneuvering, especially in this critical period when the world was trying to form a new monetary system and each major nation jockeyed for support of its positions.

Consequently, the IMF meeting at Nairobi became more a forum for discussions on the major monetary and economic issues of the day rather than the occasion for substantial progress on a new world monetary system. That goal was formally postponed until July, 1974. The Committee of 20 scheduled its next meeting for January, 1974 in Rome and planned to continue its efforts to come up with a new proposal now that the major issues were defined. The floating went on as usual and a period of stability returned to currency markets.

World Economic Crisis

Stability was not the word to describe the world at large for the remainder of 1973. War between the Arabs and Israelis in October, 1973, followed by an Arab oil embargo and a 300% increase in the world price of oil created military, political and economic havoc. Whereas currency problems could be handled by floating, when the oil crisis emerged, the industrial nations of the world were without readily available alternatives. The focus of the world turned to the urgent oil and energy problems associated with the Middle Eastern situation.

These military, political and economic events had a sharp impact on the world's monetary system in the following three ways:

(1) The oil price increase tended to fall with varying weight on different nations, affecting their inflation rates, economic prosperity and trade and payment balances. The nearly quadrupled cost of crude oil "heated up" inflation in an already inflation-prone world caus-

ing deepening recessions in national economies already strained by shortages, inflation and the financing of vastly escalated balance of payments deficits. In face of these critical problems international cooperation and free trade were in danger of being swept aside by protectionist national economic policies, competitive devaluations and trade and capital controls.

(2) International monetary flows were changed. Greatly increased oil prices channeled huge amounts of currency to the OPEC nations and the ability of the world monetary system to handle this new flow was in question. With almost all of the non-Communist world's industrial nations absolutely dependent on the OPEC nations for oil, the massive trade and payment deficits of the industrial nations were matched by massive trade and payment surpluses of the OPEC nations. Concern arose as to what the OPEC nations would do with their surpluses and how that might change world capital markets and currency values.

The size of the projected surpluses of the OPEC nations staggered monetary leaders who foresaw the tremendous impact on currency values of simple OPEC decisions to switch their funds from one currency to another. A bigger concern was the ability of world capital markets to recycle the huge surpluses, especially to those nations needing outside financing in order to pay their oil bills. The burden of these circumstances fell hardest on the small, underdeveloped nations, whose absolute dependence on outside oil coupled with a lack of attractive investment opportunities in their nations created great economic problems. How to get the additional funds to these nations became an urgent problem.

(3) International monetary reform and the progress toward it were certainly hindered by these events. The IMF Committee of 20 met in Rome in January, 1974, amidst the most pressing of economic circumstances.

The massive accumulations of funds projected for the OPEC nations made any consideration of a return to a fixed rate monetary system unthinkable. Considering the urgent economic problems facing the nations, any idea of forging ahead now on any new system was equally ridiculous. In effect, the work of the Committee of 20 was usurped by the OPEC ministers who made the floating system more permanent by their actions. Much of the discussion in Rome focused on the role of the IMF in helping nations finance their new oil bills and in channeling OPEC surplus funds into valid investment opportunities. The float was continued indefinitely in the face of these other, more pressing issues.

The Bleak Winter of 1974

The winter of 1973-1974 was economically bleak. Except for two changes in the value of two major currencies, the area of monetary affairs was quiet:

(1) In January, 1974, there was a de facto devaluation of the Japanese yen, which provided an interesting example of how a dirty float operates and how the new economic relationships produced by the energy crisis affected currency values. Since 1971 the yen had been stronger than the dollar due to the favorable Japanese trade and payment balances. As a result, the dollar gradually slipped against the yen until their values stabilized in the summer of 1973. But Japan depended more heavily on OPEC oil than did the U.S. and thus was harder hit economically by the increased price. The dollar began to rise in value against the yen. In the manner of the dirty float, the Japanese central bank helped the yen by intervening in currency markets, selling U.S. dollars for yen to keep the yen-dollar relationship within the limits desired by Japanese monetary officials. Finally, after a period

of massive intervention, the Japanese gave up. They accepted the rise of the dollar and, in effect, devalued the yen by doing nothing. The dollar rose against the yen and produced a 6-7% devaluation (or more realistically depreciation) of the yen, which stabilized on the market at approximately 300 to the dollar. By changing its intervention points, the Japanese central bank changed the limits on the float of the yen. This was the way the managed float operated.

(2) As discussed earlier, in January, 1974, the French withdrew from the European joint float and allowed the "commercial franc" to float alone causing it to decline in value.

Exit the Committee of 20

One of the few formal and agreed upon outcomes of the Nairobi IMF annual meeting was a postponement of the goal of monetary reform until July, 1974. The Committee of 20 continued to work toward this deadline but after its January, 1974 meeting in Rome, any major revision of the current system of floating was hopeless. The Committee did, however, meet as scheduled in Washington in June, 1974 and as expected concentrated on efforts to make the existing floating system work better. But the June meeting, too, was overshadowed by OPEC, as the OPEC ministers planned to meet in Ecuador the following week to discuss another round of oil price increases! The Committee's actions added further legitimacy and permanence to the floating and it was generally concluded that any change from this "interim" system would require a long evolutionary process.

In matters of substance, the Committee agreed upon the following steps to help make the float more "manageable and stable".

(1) A new scheme was adopted revaluing the SDR

at the average value of a "basket" of 16 currencies rather than just the dollar. This move added
greater stability to the value of the SDR and eventually led to a number of commercial applications of
the SDR, as we shall see in Chapter IV.

(2) Guidelines were presented to govern the timing
and techniques of governmental intervention in the currency markets to influence the value of their currencies.

(3) A pledge was drawn up for IMF member nations to refrain from adopting protectionist trade and
currency actions during the float.

(4) A plan was presented to set up a new IMF committee to replace the Committee of 20 and to continue the effort toward monetary reform.

With this work done and its last meeting held,
after a very long and difficult tenure, the Committee
of 20 dissolved. It would eventually be replaced
by an Interim Committee of 20 which would continue the work.

It should be noted here that the Group of 10
finance ministers also met at this time and reached
agreement on a plan to allow nations to use the market value of their national gold stocks as collateral
for loans. This is discussed in greater detail in Chap-
tert IV.

The Lull in Monetary Developments

The general and widespread economic aftermath
of the inflation and energy crisis brought a recession
which began to affect the major nations of the world
in 1974. One country after another found itself in an
economic slump with little appreciation for the form of
an international monetary system compared with the
far more pressing question of how to combat inflation
and recession. Although competitive devaluation and
protectionist international trade policies were tempting
to use, they were declared off limits and most nations

avoided using them. In fact, had they tried they would not have been very successful, since one nation openly resorting to these tactics would have touched off a trade and currency war, potentially world-wide, in which every nation could end up losing.

During this period, floating continued relatively crisis free and stable. Some excitement in monetary circles was stirred by large exchange losses suffered by a few major banks from speculation (authorized and unauthorized). But this did not turn out to be as widespread as initially feared. A number of events related to monetary gold occurred which will be discussed later in the book. During this "lull" in monetary developments, there was time to analyze the floating experience and to raise questions about the future direction of world monetary progress. The assumption since 1973 had been that floating was a temporary measure to be replaced with a better operating fixed rate system. Now, this assumption was re-examined in light of the recent experience with floating and the contemporary international economic situation.

A number of papers on the situation in monetary affairs and proposals for the future appeared in the financial press and these too are presented in Chapter III. During this period, monetary negotiations continued, but less visibly. The Interim Committee was not as publicly active in pursuing monetary progress as the previous Committee of 20, which had regularly scheduled meetings, communiques . and press conferences. In addition, behind the scenes negotiations by leading monetary officials of the major nations tended to be secret. By the summer of 1975, there was open concern about the lull in progress toward monetary reform, especially from those who believed that floating was not the optimal system. There were questions too about the lack of official concern by the IMF about these matters.

The Wall Street Journal posed some of these

very questions to Secretary of the Treasury William E. Simon, in an editorial in June, 1975. The editorial, Mr. Simon's answer, and the response of the editorial staff to Mr. Simon in another editorial are presented as Reading 4. This dialogue provides valuable insights into contemporary monetary thinking, the American position on the major monetary issues of the day and what future developments were anticipated. In addition, Secretary Simon, in discussing the recent past period of monetary negotiations from his vantage point, provides an illuminating view as to what was happening.

READING 4

The Vacancy at Treasury

A Treasury Secretary has to wear many hats. He has to defend the administration's economic policy in general. He has to concern himself with debt management, with energy policy, with the condition of the trust funds, with tax policy. He negotiates with other finance ministers on issues of trade, aid and tariffs.

For a year now, William Simon has worn most of these hats, with exuberance, even panache, and we have agreed with his positions more often than not. But there is one important hat a Treasury Secretary should be wearing that Mr. Simon has refused to don. He has shown absolutely no interest in international monetary reform, and for all we know those offices at Treasury that should be peopled with monetary technicians and architects have been vacant for a year.

His argument has been that global economic conditions are so turbulent and economic thinking in global capitals so diverse that it would be impossible anyway to get an agreement on a rebuilt monetary system. Jack F. Bennett, his Under Secretary for Monetary Affairs, pins the blame on the French, whom he accuses of having an "extreme" position on the future monetary role of gold. But to Mr. Bennett, any monetary role for gold is an extreme, so it is hardly surprising that the French doubt an agreement can ever be reached as long as the U.S. is represented by Mr. Bennett.

Nor do we have any sense that if Secretary Simon were elevated to the position of global dictator, and could impose a monetary system even the French would meekly have to accept, he would have anything in mind at all. What is the Treasury design? Is there a blueprint, even a penciled sketch? Would he insist on a "clean" floating of exchange rates, with any central banker who intervened on behalf of his currency put before a firing squad? Would he impose a system of absolutely fixed rates, with any central banker who ran a deficit through excessive monetary expansion boiled in oil? Would he control Eurodollars? Eurocurrencies? What would he do with the mountains of gold now held by central banks?

There certainly must be a better way to run a world monetary system, to everyone's benefit, than the current non-system. Floating exchange rates have had the virtue of working during a time in which there has been no international system, but they have thoroughly failed to live up to their once-trumpeted *theoretical* virtues. Their one-time proponents are at a total loss in explaining why the currency markets have gyrated so wildly. Floating, we all recall, was supposed to have brought glacial adjustments in exchange rates that would gradually shift trade flows and solve every nation's balance of payments problems.

More importantly, it is a raw fact that the era of floating rates has also been an era of explosive inflation, and now recession, in the Western economies. While the causation can be debated, clearly a floating regime has done nothing to solve the problem. Nor have trade flows been especially responsive to exchange-rate changes; witness the continuing West German surpluses despite constant appreciation of the mark. It is as if, as Arthur Laffer argued on this page two years ago, trade balances and exchange rates are completely independent of each other.

At the time Mr. Simon became Treasury Secretary, it was asserted that monetary reform was unlikely unless and until the United States got inflation under control. Now, of course the U.S. needs to get inflation under control, and more pertinently keep it under control, for both domestic and international reasons. But there are reasons to doubt that this is possible without at least some minimum international agreement to regulate presently unchecked money creation in the Eurodollar market. And in any event, the existence of inflation then, or recession now, is no reason to avoid thinking about the international arena—or to leave international economic policy to the tender mercies of the State Department.

There may never be a right time to get

started on international reform; in fact, the lack of reform may be what is preventing a right time. As much as we admire Mr. Simon, his international monetary hatlessness has gone on long enough.

Treasury Secretary Simon Replies

Editor, the Wall Street Journal:

As you know, I have taken encouragement from many of your editorials but I am disappointed and puzzled by the positions—and the inaccuracies—in your editorials of May 29 on "The Vacancy at the Treasury" and "The Paper Blizzard."

For some time I have known that at least one of your Editorial Board believes that we should attempt to return to a rigid, gold-based international monetary system. I am convinced that, in practice, any such attempt would prove disruptive of international trade and investment and damaging to the U.S. and foreign economies.

I favor a different approach. Specifically, I am working for the adoption of a more flexible system, one which reflects the diversity of the real world, and allows nations greater freedom of choice in specific exchange rate arrangements, provided they act in accordance with an agreed code of international behavior. Additionally, I am working for a system in which the role of gold is reduced, in order to lessen the destabilizing effects of that commodity on the monetary system. This objective is widely shared, and the International Monetary Fund's ministerial Interim

Committee has formally agreed to seek arrangements "to ensure that the role of gold in the international monetary system would be gradually reduced."

Some may feel that the term "international monetary reform" can only be applied to a full, one-shot introduction of a comprehensive new system of rules. My own judgment is, however, that any attempt at a sudden adoption of a brave new international monetary world would, in practice, prove both impermanent and disruptive. I am convinced far better results will come from less glamorous efforts to guide gradual evolution of the system as widespread consensus can be attained. Meanwhile, the combination of flexible rates and informal intergovernmental consultations developed over the last several years has worked remarkably well considering the shocks the international economy has been subjected to during that period by the embargo and cutbacks in oil production, by economic boom and recession, and by widely disparate rates of inflation in the different countries.

U.S. international monetary policy must fit into a comprehensive effort simultaneously to restore economic growth and price stability, to adapt to the energy shocks in ways that will support a pattern of orderly growth, and to accommodate to massive shifts in international financial flows. I believe U.S. international monetary policy has fitted into such a comprehensive approach.

Our analyses of recent experience may differ, but our differences in this regard should not cause you to be blind to the strenuous efforts we in the Treasury have been making to negotiate gradual improvements in international monetary arrangements.

Outstanding Individuals

I was disappointed by your misleading statement that "for all we know those offices at Treasury that should be peopled with monetary technicians and architects have been vacant for a year." In fact, throughout my time as Secretary it has been my good fortune that the key international monetary posts in the Treasury have been occupied by outstanding individuals well equipped for their important assignments with a combination of both academic and practical experience at home and abroad. These now include such men as Jack Bennett, Charles Cooper, Sam Cross and Lisle Widman.

You say that I have "shown absolutely no interest in international monetary reform." Yet the record will show that I have spent many days on the subject both in Washington and on my 10 trips abroad during the past year. Just within that period I have attended nine formal international ministerial meetings on the subject, in addition to numerous informal sessions with key ministers of other nations.

The unfairness of your editorials' charge of neglect of international monetary affairs probably seems particularly acute to me now, since I have just returned from monetary discussions in Paris and will be going back on Sunday for a week of further discussions with finance ministers' in Paris and with private U.S. and foreign bankers in Amsterdam.

In part, your allegation of neglect of international economics by the Treasury seems to result from your surprise that the speeches of the Secretary of State have dealt exclusively and seriously with the economic aspects of our international relations. I certainly find it neither surprising nor inappropriate that our government recognizes the fundamental importance of economic developments in world affairs, and I would like to assure you that Secretary Kissinger has on no occasion made a major address containing significant economic paragraphs without first discussing those paragraphs with me.

Contrary to the impression given by your editorials, there are some accomplishments to show from the negotiations among the finance ministers over the past year. Agreement has been reached among the OECD nations to establish a $25 billion safety net to assist any member facing serious financial difficulty as a result of the economic forces unleashed by the abrupt cutback in supply from the traditional suppliers of much of the world's oil. Special arrangements were agreed within the IMF to help meet the financing needs of member nations whose oil import costs have risen sharply. Agreement has been reached on the outlines of a one-third increase in the quotas for members of the International Monetary Fund. The IMF Interim Committee and IMF-IBRD Development Committee were established. Guidelines for floating were adopted. And a new method of valuation of the SDR was agreed.

In addition, work has been commissioned on design of additional facilities to assist those less developed countries most seriously affected by the recent vast changes in commodity price structures. Moreover, agreement in principle has been reached that the gradual phase-down in the official monetary role of gold will be achieved in a manner which does not force the immobilization of the assets held by governments and the IMF in the form of gold.

Difficult and important negotiations still do lie ahead. The Articles of Agreement of the IMF now literally require every member to maintain a par value for its currency and that solemn obligation is being violated by every member of the fund: and, yet, we still have not reached agreement on how to replace that provision by a new provision more persuasive of practical cooperation among governments in avoiding disorderly exchange market conditions. At the same time, as we seek to relax the constraints on the uses of official holdings of gold, we still have not reached agreement on the exact safeguards which should be put in place to insure against any drift back toward the dangerous brittleness of attempted fixed relationships between currencies and gold. Nevertheless, I am hopeful that if the negotiations can be all in a spirit of realism, agreement can be reached soon.

Meanwhile, the world economy is benefiting from the changes already achieved in introducing greater flexibility into our international monetary arrangements. I definitely do not agree with your contention that the experience suggests that "trade balances and exchange rates are completely independent of each other." This hypothesis has been carefully examined by numerous economists, both in and outside the government. The preponderant majority of their studies—while recognizing that trade flows are also influenced by fiscal and monetary policies and by cyclical factors—confirm the common sense notion that exchange rate changes do have an important impact on trade flows.

For confirmation one need only look at the substantial improvement in the United States non-oil trade balance since the dollar was de-valued. Our oil import costs have, of course, risen dramatically for reasons unrelated to the exchange rate for the dollar. But the balance in our trade in all items other than oil has changed dramatically since the devaluations, from a deficit of $2.7 billion in 1972 to a surplus of $18.3 billion in 1974. You mention continued West German trade surpluses despite constant appreciation of the mark, but you don't men-tion much of the mark's appreciation has re-flected the comparatively exemplary West Ger-man performance in holding down its rate of money and price inflation. Nor do you mention the intense concern which has now developed in West Germany over the decline in export orders as Germany's large basic balance surplus has turned into a deficit.

I also cannot accept your description of the U.S. dollar as a "weak instrument" internation-ally. When the dollar is judged appropriately in relation to a relevant weighted average of other currencies, its value has increased about 3% over the past three months; it is stronger today than it was a year ago; and its value today is almost exactly what it was in early 1973, when generalized floating of currencies began.

Over this period, the dollar certainly has not, to use your phrase, gyrated wildly. Over the past year, its trade weighted value would have been contained within a range of plus or minus 3.1%, and since early 1973 within a range of only 4.6%. During this period the dollar has been the most stable of the world's five major currencies, but I would not apply the term "gyrating wildly" to any of them.

The Basic Problem

I cannot agree with you either that the major economic problems of the world have their origin "in a single source, the instability of world currencies." It seems to me that you are attacking the symptoms rather than the sources. It would be more in line with your usual perceptiveness if you concentrated attention not on the alleged instability among currencies but rather on the extent of the excessive creation of currency and government debt in all major countries in recent years.

This is a basic problem which must be faced head-on by our political institutions, and there is no simple gimmick which will provide an easy solution. In particular, any attempt in today's world to try to slow the printing presses by trying to link currencies to gold would only exacerbate the problem. It would probably lead on quickly to a combination of government controls, which would undermine the increased production we need to fight inflation, and of repeated jumps of exchange rate revaluation, whose very discontinuity could not fail to disrupt beneficial international investment and trade. Moreover, fixed exchange rates would undermine the efforts of those nations trying harder to restrain inflation by making it harder for them to avoid importing the effects of the higher inflation in other countries.

The answer—the only answer—is to achieve a wider public understanding of the dangers of legislating public expenditures far in excess of public revenues. You can help get the answer recognized.

> **WILLIAM E. SIMON**
> *Secretary of the Treasury*
> *Washington*

World Monetary Reform: A Primer

In Treasury Secretary Simon's response to our editorials suggesting Treasury has no international economic policy, there runs an implicit question the Secretary was too courteous to put explicitly: Just what international monetary policy does The Wall Street Journal think the Treasury ought to have?

It is a mildly embarrassing question for the truth is that our own ideas have been in considerable ferment over the last few years. Initially we were reasonably receptive to the advent of floating exchange rates, but since their actual advent the world economy some how does not look healthier. World inflation has been higher, and now world recession has been sharper. Since Secretary Simon now assures us that the 1971 ideas he describes alongside are still definitive, we should perhaps amend our criticism. It is not that Treasury has no position; rather, it has a position oblivious to experience. Our recent experience *should* cause ferment and questioning, and perhaps it would be well to put down some partial conclusions of our own.

(1) Secretary Simon is absolutely on target when he says the root problem is the creation of money. It was excessive money creation that caused the huge world inflation, and the current recession is the inevitable correction. We think, though, that Treasury needs to face squarely the question of whether money is created not only by central banks but also in the Eurodollar market, for if that is true a more structured international monetary system is inevitably necessary. But in any event, the choice of fixed or floating rates and the role for gold are subsidiary questions. They are alternative weapons in the main battle, which is keeping money creation in line with production of goods and services.

(2) In terms of pure economics, the ideal system would be one world currency controlled by one central bank devoted to correct monetary growth. A common currency would facilitate the market efficiencies that maximize production and wealth; this maximizing is the secret of the success of large trading areas such as the continent-spanning United States. We assume that not even Under Secretary Bennett would argue for floating rates between the Federal Reserve Bank of New York and the Federal Reserve BAnk of San Francisco. Of course, in the real world, a single central bank is probably as illusory as a world goverment.

(3) If it were possible to have firmly fixed rates, however, you would in effect have one world currency going by different names in different countries. To maintain fixed rates over any length of time, different central banks wouild have to devote their monetary policies

largely to that objective. They would all have to inflate at the same rate. This in effect was how the pure gold standard worked, wittingly or not; the gain or loss of gold reserves would expand or contract the money supply of individual nations, while additions to the supply of gold controlled world money growth. With a true consensus among governments, you theoretically would do the same thing with any international reserve—gold, moonrocks, or even special drawing rights.

(4) In theory, the advantage floating rates were supposed to offer was the opportunity for each nation to run its own monetary policy independently of international conditions, thus choosing its own inflation rate. In practice this advantage has proved highly illusory. Germany has been able to keep its inflation rate below that of other nations, but it has been forced to accept more inflation than it wanted. In practice, it has not been able to isolate itself from the world inflation. Nor have floating rates adjusted away the trade surpluses of Germany or deficits of Britain.

(5) On second look, this result is not even theoretically surprising. Even under floating rates, corporate treasurers and others can choose to hold their balances in one currency or another, and are sensitive to interest rates. This means that interest rates in Germany are not independent of interest rates in the United States, which in turn limits the independence of monetary policy.

Nor is it surprising that devaluing a currency does not improve a trade balance. Currencies are essentially the yardsticks by which we measure relative prices; regardless of the value of the dollar versus the guilder, a pound to copper mined in Utah still will buy the same hunk of Dutch cheese. What happens instead is that the yardsticks readjust, through changes in nominal prices of copper and cheese in the two currencies. Practially all economists agree that this is true in the long run; the argument is over how rapidly the effect takes place, in particular for non-traded goods and services. If the adjustment takes place in the short run, there is not even a temporary trading advantage in a depreciating currency.

(6) We live in a world economy increasingly integrated by advances in communications and the advent of multinational firms. To move someone's bank balance, Chase can talk to Barclays as easily as it can talk to Chemical. ITT can, if it chooses, borrow just as conveniently in Zurich as in New York. Whatever time adjustments used to take, they must take much less now.

(7) If central banks believe they have independence of monetary policy but do not in fact have it, the system will show signs of instability. If each bank follows only domestic targets, oblivious to the effect on its own economy or the actions of foreign central banks, the total effect is likely to be overreaction. You could have, for example, a swing of especially virulent world inflation followed by an unexpectedly virulent world recession. Avoiding this is called coordinating monetary policies; one way to coordinate monetary policies is to fix rates.

(8) Modern democracies have an inflationary bias, and this is reflected in their international system. Yale economist Robert Triffin

points out that the official reserves of central banks, on which domestic money creation is based, exploded to $209 billion in 1974 from $78 billion in 1970. The oil cartel put itself at the head of the line, but the fundamental cause of the inflation still lies in excessive money growth.

(9) A great deal of the argument, and the ultimate point raised by Secretary Simon, is which problem you cure first. The burst of world inflation, traceable largely to U.S. monetary policies after 1965, broke up the Bretton Woods system. Unless the developed nations can first cure their inflationary bias, the argument runs, they cannot subject their monetary policies to the discipline of maintaining fixed rates The true consensus necessary to fixed rates does not presently exist, and any new system of fixed rates would quickly break down, which is clearly worse than the float.

This may be true, but it is our impression that the chief place the necessary consensus is lacking is the United States in general and the Treasury in particular. Even without some massive new system, a great deal could be done simply by fixing the dollar to the mark—not in the long run by massive support operations but by adjusting monetary policies. In Paris last week, the Europeans apparently proposed essentially this, and the U.S. rejected it.

It is further our guess that if a new system of fixed rates did break down, the chief offender would be the United States. It would be the U.S. that would insist on expanding its money supply faster than the rest of the world. And this is what puzzles us about Secretary

Simon. He is solidly for restrained money growth in the U.S., and in its support he is willing to use every conceivable argument except one: That we and the other developed nations are locked into a complicated system none of us can manage independently, and our responsibility to collective management is to keep money growth moderate.

It may be true that the developed world currently lacks the political will to run anything similar to the Bretton Woods system that served their economies so well for so many years. But the position we would like to see at Treasury is one that seeks to build that will rather than destroy it. At the very least, in the light of what has happened to the world economy over the last few years, the time has long since passed to apotheosize floating rates.

The 1975 annual meeting of the IMF was held in early September in Washington, D.C. Most of the actions taken were related to gold and are covered in detail in Chapter IV. The meeting was preceded by meetings of the IMF's Monetary Negotiations Committee, consisting of 20 finance ministers, with concurrent meetings of the finance ministers of the Group of 10. The IMF Committee reached agreement on a proposed sale of IMF gold to benefit the poor nations but this proposal was contingent on the ability of the Interim Committee of 20 to reach agreement on currency matters at its Jamaica meeting in January, 1976. The Group of 10 ministers also reached agreement on related gold matters. The principal non-gold action was a proposal to modify the voting power within the IMF to give greater power to OPEC and Third World nations.

The Way to Rambouillet

By the fall of 1975, the major industrial nations of the world faced such a broad spectrum of national economic problems (energy, inflation and recession) that an economic summit meeting was called. For three days in November, 1975 at a chateau in Rambouillet, France, ranking officials of Japan, Italy, France, West Germany, Great Britain, and the U.S. (represented by President Ford, Secretary of State Henry Kissinger, and Secretary of the Treasury William E. Simon) met to consider how they might cooperate to their mutual benefit.

International monetary relationships was a major topic on the agenda, thereby making Rambouillet an international monetary conference at the highest level. It also reflected a changed form of negotiations in that it was carried out by the world leaders, personally, rather than through representatives of the IMF. Not, of course that the meeting was independent of the IMF or unrelated to IMF concerns—but on the other hand, a movement away from channeling all monetary negotiations through the IMF is evident.

On the monetary front, the French and the Americans held opposing views going into Rambouillet. The French had long sought a return to the pattern of monetary affairs of the immediate past: fixed rates and dollar convertibility; whereas the American position was to continue the status quo: floating and no dollar convertibility. The scene was set for a dramatic confrontation. But in terms of concrete monetary developments at Rambouillet, there really weren't any. The monetary world was set to buzzing at an early report of an agreement at Rambouillet to return to a kind of fixed rate system through much greater internationally coordinated central bank intervention in the float, but the official statements later showed this to be in error.

The 17-point declaration issued by the conference after its conclusion had the following monetary ramifications:

(1) the nations agreed to "work for greater stability" in currency rates but no specific actions to achieve this were announced.

(2) the monetary authorities agreed to continue to intervene in the float but called for "smoothing" actions, meant to counter the effect of disorderly market conditions or erratic fluctuations in rates.

(3) the conference pointed out that a major source of stability in exchange rates would be the underlying economic stability in the national economies themselves and this was a major thrust of the conference. In fact, the conference showed a strong spirit of agreement and cooperation among the major nations to work together to see to it that the world would recover from the recession without a new dose of double-digit inflation. This "new spirit" was to boost the confidence of the world in the immediate economic future.

From the viewpoint of monetary affairs, the Rambouillet summit limited itself to endorsing the status quo, and defining it better. In a sense, the French were defeated (or compromised, depending on your position) in the negotiations. Reading 5 on the following page is the evaluation and commentary on the Rambouillet meeting, by the editors of the *Journal* who welcomed the new spirit of cooperation and saw great potential in it.

READING 5

The Significance of Rambouillet

We've now had a few days to read between the lines of the communique from last weekend's economic summit meeting in Rambouillet, France. Having done so, we can write with some confidence that the agreements by the six heads of the West's chief industrial nations are potentially of the highest order of importance.

The agreements express a desire to coordinate the economic policies of the industrial nations, and provide a number of forums for this purpose. As a token of the seriousness of intent and a guide to its eventual evolution, the agreements provide explicit rules for an eventual return to fixed exchange rate parities. In essence this means that the major nations—and above all the United States—have abandoned the wishful idea of totally autonomous monetary policies that has animated the recent experiment with floating rates.

Yes, Treasury Secretary Simon says nothing much has really changed, that the dollar would continue to float. Governments will intervene, perhaps, to counter "irrational" swings in currency values, but won't try to offset fluctuations that reflect "underlying economic circumstances." But if you cut thorugh the fog, what this means is that the United States will use its reserves to stabilize the dollars only if it decides—through consultation with theother governments—that the fluctuations are occurring thorugh speculative excesses.

Of greater significance is the one passage of the communique that reads: "With regard to monetary problems, we affirm our intention to work for greater stability. This involves efforts to restore greater stability in underlying economic and financial conditions." This could be diplomatic pap. But if it means anything at all, it means the respective governments will make an effort to stabilize exchange rates by adjusting their monetary policies.

If this is done, it insures coordination of monetary policy in all of the economies. If for one reason or another a country prints too much of its currency its exchange rate will come under pressure, signaling the need to slow down the presses. This coordination—and if the consultation is successful, restraint—of monetary policy is the essence and purpose of a fixed-rate system. The rates (under a float) or reserves (under fixed parities) are the thermometers.

This has been forgotten in recent years, but ever since disenchantment with the floating experiment began setting in, it's been absolutely clear that a return to a stable system would have to involve more than the old methods of currency intervention. Bretton Woods broke down, and a world inflation ensued, because nations—particularly the United States, but also at times Britain and France—attempted to divorce domestic monetary policies from international exchange rate policy.

Countries would defend the par value of their currency by buying it when it weakened and selling it when it strengthened, but if they were printing up money at home faster than they could mop it up on the exchange market, reserves would be depleted and devaluation was the only option.

The "rapprochement" between the six nations at Rambouillet suggests there has been a fundamental commitment of each to use both international reserves and domestic monetary tools, such as Federal Reserve open-market operations, to see if rates can be stabilized in a politically acceptable fashion. Indeed, Eugene Birnbaum of First National Bank of Chicago suspects a broad attempt of this nature to stabilize the dollar-Deutschemark rate has been under way since mid-October, there being only trivial fluctuations in that rate for several weeks.

The hesitation of the Rambouillet participants in explaining that this is what they have in mind is understandable. While there seems to have been a conceptual breakthrough that has permitted earlier differences to be composed, there are no doubt remaining differences even in the interpretation of what the communique itself amounts to. Everyone seems to agree an embryo of an idea has been conceived at the summit, but nobody can say for sure what it will look like if and when it grows up.

In January, when the IMF interim committee meets in Jamaica, there should be clearer indications of where the West may be headed on monetary reform, and whether our current optimistic reading is warranted. If our reading is correct, and the embryo can successfully mature in a cruel world of divergent national politics, Rambouillet may prove to be a beginning towards control of global inflation.

The Jamaica IMF

Two months after the Rambouillet economic summit, the International Monetary Fund held a formal meeting of the Interim Committee of 20. Ten representatives of major industrial nations and 10 representatives of developing Third World nations met in Jamaica to work on proposals to be submitted to the IMF member nations for ratification in 1976. It turned out to be a first rate forum for international monetary news and developments.

Since Nairobi, the nature of monetary negotiations had been broadened to include related economic issues. As they gathered in Jamaica, the Committee's agenda included the following:

(1) The structure of the world monetary system. Although currency rates had been floating since 1973, according to the IMF rules floating was not officially recognized. The Interim Committee faced the tricky issue of recognizing the reality of the floating without officially ruling out a return to a system of fixed rates and thereby offending its advocates, mostly notably the French. After a week of meetings and negotiations, the Committee approved a recommendation to amend the IMF Charter by adding a new article, IV "Obligations Regarding Exchange Arrangement." It represented official IMF recognition of the floating system currently in effect, but also committed the IMF to continue efforts toward monetary reform. It encouraged member nations to achieve stable economic growth and thus contribute toward exchange rate stability. And it permitted nations to adopt fixed rates for their currencies, defining par value in terms of the SDR. Details concerning the setting of the initial par value, its maintenance through governmental intervention (with a proposed band of plus or minus 4.5%) and procedures for subsequent changes

in the par value were also proposed. The proposed amendment to the IMF charter also contained the provision that the IMF could decide to reinstate a fixed rate system if 85% of the membership agreed. All in all, it was a comprehensive proposal. The details were specific and can be found in Appendix C. The French hand in writing them is evident.

(2) Financial Assistance to Needy Nations. This issue, raised in Nairobi in 1974, was still being discussed by the IMF. It became the most hotly debated and controversial issue on the Interim Committee's agenda, overshadowing the currency related issues. It essentially involved two basic actions: (a) The proposed sale of 25 million ounces of IMF gold over the next four years with the profit (measured by the difference between the selling price and the official value of ($42.22) going into a fund to provide aid for poor nations; and (b) A proposal to finance their balance of payment problems, still caused mainly by the increased cost of oil. Ultimate agreement was reached within the week on both issues but ratification by the IMF was expected to take much longer.

After being agreed upon at Jamaica, these proposals would be presented to the Board of Governors of the IMF in April, then be submitted to the 128 member nations of the IMF. Ratification required approval by three-fifths of the members or 77 nations.

The proposed package of financial aid created a controversy when it was announced by the Interim Committee but the proposed amendment to the IMF Charter recognizing the legitimacy of the float and assigning a key role to the SDR was of greater significance. The majority of the points in the proposed amendment concerning the float were similar to the agreements reached at Rambouillet. But so sweeping were these currency-related proposals that the work of the Interim Committee was called "a new Bretton Woods" by Secretary of the Treasury William E. Simon.

The actions at the Jamaica meeting represented something of a paradox. On the one hand, the IMF was finally taking some positive action in recognizing the currency system in effect and giving its blessing to the float, a step long overdue in the absence of any plans to adopt another system in lieu of the float. But also contained in the proposed charter amendment is a strong case for fixed rates and the potential for a return to fixed rates if 85% of the IMF member nations agree. The latter needed the concurrence of the U.S, which controlled 20% of the votes, but the potential and its existence is significant.

As might be expected, the reactions to the work of the Interim Committee at Jamaica and the recent economic summit at Rambouillet were varied. Reading 6 presents two opposing views, one optimistic, by the editors of the *Journal* and the other pessimistic and anti-IMF by a guest editor for *Barron's*. Both looked at the accord that emerged from Jamaica and saw two very different things, not an uncommon happening in the area of international monetary affairs.

READING 6

A New Bretton Woods?

If all the International Monetary Fund achieved last week in Jamaica had been ratification of floating exchange rates and agreement to consult in order to smooth out "erratic" movements in exchange rates, it would not have done very much at all. Certainly Treasury Secretary Simon would have seemed foolish canonizing such a non-system as "a new Bretton Woods."

But what the agreement really does is to aim the world back in the direction of a par-value system, with a transition period of managed stability to give the central bankers a feel for the new system. If the central bankers can keep their currencies from fluctuating beyond a relatively narrow band for six months or a year—which is the transition period the French have in mind—the IMF will be able to nail down a par-value system that can be managed with confidence. In other words, a return to par values would naturally follow if the central banks succeed in coordinating their monetary policies around moderate growth in the world money supply. This would also spell an end to world inflation, a fall in long-term interest rates and economic revival throughout the Western world.

For any of these nice things to happen, of course, the transition has to work. Our optimism that it can work is based on two fragile assumptions. One is the the United States, France and West Germany are satisfied with the current exchange rates, i.e., they do not believe they are put at an intrinsic disadvantage commercially in maintaining these rates. The other is that Arthur Burns is not only wiser now than he was in 1971, as we all should be, but also that he will not be prevented by politicians from exercising this wisdom with continued monetary restraint.

For the key to stabilizing and eventually fixing exchange rates is the willingness of the rest of the world to accept the monetary policy of its most important currency, the dollar. Other nations can peg their currencies to the dollar, or a dollar substitute like the SDR, by buying and selling currencies in the short run and in the long run adjusting their monetary growth rates to prevent a permanent loss of reserves. This in effect means allowing the Fed to conduct their monetary policy as well as ours. They will only be willing to do so as long as they are assured the Fed is conducting a responsible monetary policy and is not printing surplus money that they are forced to swallow if they want to preserve exchange rates.

The Bretton Woods system blew apart because U.S. policymakers believed that output and employment could be expanded by more rapid monetary expansion, along the lines of the now discredited Phillips Curve. In pursuit of this chimera, the Federal Reserve had forced the other central banks to accept more and more price inflation. The United States finally broke the system, purposefully, believing the Phillips Curve was not working because of the par-value system. Instead of getting the desired results, all that resulted was double-digit inflation and a deep global recession.

If the fledgling international monetary reform is to avoid the fate of Bretton Woods, it has to incorporate the lessons of the last few years. The November agreement between the Americans and French at the Rambouillet summit meeting was in this spirit, and all that happened in Jamaica was a rubber-stamping of the accord negotiated by U.S. Under Secretary Edward Yeo and French Deputy Finance Minister Jacques de Larosiere. So far so good.

There have been daily consultations among the central bankers. The dollar and European currencies have been their steadiest in years. And even the British have been good. Is it possible that Rambouillet has something to do with the stock market boom throughout the West?

Our reading of Rambouillet and the IMF Jamaica meeting is admittedly quite different, and ultimately far more optimistic, than can be found elsewhere in the American press. And our analysis will be clearly proven wrong if, over the next several months, the dollar plunges sharply or climbs rapidly against the European currencies. But our fragile assumptions about the Europeans on one hand and Arthur Burns on the other seem valid enough and will hold together as long as congressional liberals don't force another Phillips Curve down the Fed's throat, by, for example, running deficits so large the Fed is forced to inflate in financing them.

Coordination of monetary policies and stabilization of exchange rates are by no means the whole answer to the world's economic difficulties. But an end to the worst of the inflation is nothing to be sneezed at, and it would free policymakers to focus without distraction on the problems of real growth and unemployment. So if the new accords do prove to be solid and lasting, Mr. Simon's characterization of them as a new Bretton Woods will be justified in full.

Sea of Red Ink

Despite Jamaica, the World's
Currencies Remain Adrift

DR. HENRY HAZLITT

When the foredoomed decisions of the Smithsonian conference were first announced in December 1971, they were hailed by then-President Nixon as "the greatest monetary agreement in the history of the world." Perhaps because of a lingering memory of such fatuity, nobody dared to say anything quite so extravagant about the new accords reached by the International Monetary Fund's Interim Committee of 20 at Jamaica early last month. Nonetheless, Secretary of the Treasury Simon called it "a new Bretton Woods." Under Secretary Yeo declared, "We have a monetary system again." Hans Apel, Finance Minister of West Germany, was heard to murmur, "All is solved."

It would be hard for a neutral observer to say precisely what was solved. The outstanding achievement of the conference allegedly is that it legalized floating exchange rates, while permitting any country wishing to return eventually to a fixed exchange rate to do so. But nearly every country was already—albeit "illegally"—on a floating exchange rate. And the world doesn't need the IMF either to prohibit or sanctify one. The truth is that no fundamental reform was achieved at Jamaica. Most of the agreements reached there a.·e more likely to stimulate inflation that contain it.

For perspective, let's glance back 32 years to 1944, when the Bretton Woods agreements were put together. The two most influential framers of their terms were John Maynard Keynes of Great Britain and Harry Dexter White of the U.S. Treasury. The result clearly reflected their peculiar ideas. They believed that the traditional gold standard was "a relic of barbarism," and that they had dreamed up a vastly superior substitute.

What they devised was a dollar-exchange system, which was not too far from what had already grown up in practice. Each currency was to be pegged to the dollar at a fixed rate. Only the dollar itself was to be made directly convertible into gold—at $35 an ounce—and convertible even then only at the request of central banks.

It was not hard to sell this scheme to spokesmen for the other 43 countries represented at Bretton Woods. They were thereby relieved of any obligation to convert their currency into gold, and could expand money and credit more freely. If they got into trouble, they had access to automatic borrowing rights from the new International Monetary Fund. The whole arrangement made it much safer to inflate.

Inflate they did. And though for a time nations in trouble were rescued by the other members, a major breakdown occurred as early as 1949. In that year the British pound was devalued by 30%—from $4.03 to $2.80—an act followed within a week by devaluations of 25 other currencies. In succeeding years there were hundreds of devaluations of currencies by members of the

Fund, but the system continued to be hailed as a great success.

Meanwhile, Congress and U.S. monetary officials took very lightly the heavy obligations they had shouldered in making the dollar the world's anchor currency. They continued to inflate the dollar supply. As a consequence, on August 15, 1971, the U.S. felt obliged to suspend the convertibility—even for central banks—of the dollar into gold. Since then, every currency has been adrift. For the first time in modern history, not a single country is doing business in a metallic money.

Surely the IMF should have been dismantled no later than the end of 1971. Instead, the machinery has been kept intact, and we get a succession of patch-up conferences, each one of which "solves all." The first "solution" this time is an increase of 45% in borrowing rights. This is put into effect by a complicated formula according to which a nation may borrow one-fourth of its "quota" with no questions asked, but with gradually stiffening conditions for the next three quarters.

What this means is that a nation's monetary managers can more safely follow inflationary policies than otherwise. For if there were no IMF to fall back on, a would-be borrower would have to convince some non-captive lender that it was solvent, likely to repay, and even willing to offer a premium interest rate to compensate for the risk. There would have been nothing like the appalling rates of inflation we have seen if such a system had existed over the past thirty years.

Having proven incapable of fulfilling its original purpose, to stabilize national currencies—and having worked to do the opposite—the IMF now is to be turned into an international charity institution. It is to sell off one-sixth of its gold on the free market, and use the profits to help the world's poorest countries.

This extends to the international field the pernicious theory that the poverty of the poor is a consequence of the wealth of the better-off. In any case, it implies that the solution is the socialistic one of redistribution, rather than the capitalistic one of increasing production.

The Jamaica accords have futher inflationary tendencies. Not only is gold to be phased out, but also the Special Drawing Right—i.e., irredeemable paper money, or bookkeeping credit created out of thin air—is to become "the principal reserve asset in the international monetary system."

Yet in the new agreement there may prove to be an unintended silver lining—or should we say a golden one? The IMF will sell off gold. But there is more than a hint that most of its holdings are likely to end up either in the vaults of the Bank for International Settlements or those of the world's central banks. Either way, it will then be in hands that will appreciate its value more than the chrysophobic bureaucrats who run the IMF. Let us remember that the avowed purpose of the IMF from the very beginning was to "phase gold out" of the monetary system.

In addition, it is clearly stipulated in the

Jamaica agreement that the Fund will be given the power "to restitute to all members, on the basis of present quotas and at the present official price, any part of the gold left after the disposition of the 50 million ounces" sold to raise money for the poor nations. Once individual central banks get back their gold contributions, it will be much easier to dismantle the IMF and return eventually to a gold standard. It will also be much easier for individual nations, meanwhile, to permit their own citizens to make voluntary contracts providing for payment in gold or in terms of gold value. In view of these possibilities, long-range prospects for bullion seem considerably brighter than the recent market decline suggests.

The harm done by the IMF is not merely that it completely fails to deal with the root causes of inflation, or even that it has inflationary tendencies of its own, but that it deflects attention from the real causes of and the genuine remedy for inflation. Inflation and depreciation of a currency are always caused primarily by domestic overissuance of that currency. Such overissuance, in turn, results from that nation's own fiscal and monetary policies. Real reform must begin and end at home.

The problem will be formidable enough even after we can get this much understood. For the longer inflationary policies have been pursued, and the worse they have been, the greater the vested interest becomes in keeping them going at nearly any cost. It is less that politicians do not understand what needs to be done, than that they do not want to.

So they embrace or invent theories that call for still more inflation.

The process is nowhere better illustrated than in this country. President Ford considers it virtuous that he is proposing to spend "only" $394 billion (which would be the highest figure on record) in fiscal 1977, and that he looks for a deficit of only $43 billion. (No one, incidentally, expects either figure to be that low.) He does not plan a balanced budget. The most he promises is that his spending and tax proposals "will set us on a course that . . . leads to a balanced budget within three years." Nothing in the present Washington climate makes such an outcome likely.

But the political opposition is far worse. Senator Muskie, selected as Congressional spokesman for the Democrats, argues that the President, in trying to make even his timid approach toward a balanced budget, is being "penny-wise and pound-foolish." Muskie insists that every American must be guaranteed "a decent job and secure retirement," and implies that any attempt at federal economy must increase unemployment. Such "reasoning" implies that as long as there is any unemployment whatsoever, it will not be the time to balance the budget or even to reduce the most appalling deficit.

With pro-inflation arguments of this kind now rampant nearly everywhere, it will be hard enough to get individual nations back on the path of fiscal and monetary sanity. We only make the task still more arduous as long as we continue to support an institution like the IMF, which has become a global engine of inflation.

Post Jamaica: Crisis Rather Than Calm

Most of the optimism generated by Rambouillet and Jamaica was, basically, faith in a new spirit of cooperation which produced confidence in the currency markets. But subsequent events and certain hard realities sometimes replaced cooperation with acts of self defense. Early in 1976 international monetary developments were of this latter type. Two major problems developed:

(1) The Lira Crisis: Italy had long been in bad economic shape and the other EEC nations did what they could to help Italy establish a stable government, economy, and currency. However, all that came crashing down in January, 1976 when the Italian government fell. Previously there was tremendous selling of the Italian lira which put much pressure on the snake and introduced uncertainty into the previously calm floating markets. Those advocating a return to fixed rates again stepped up their attacks on the volatility of the float and as if to illustrate their point, the American dollar shot up from 686 lira to 733 in a short period. Exchange markets in Italy were closed for a time.

(2) Pound Problems: The second European cur-

rency to face crisis was the pound sterling. England had been badly hit by the recession and by increased oil prices. As the U.K.'s trade and payment deficits increased and domestic economic unrest developed in England, speculators put downward pressure on the pound forcing the Bank of England to intervene and support the pound. Many considered $2 to be the lower limit of the pound's float, but on Friday, March 5, 1976, the pound closed at $1.9845, then continued to drop in value on Monday. Many saw this as a British move toward competitve devaluation, by withdrawing support from the pound to allow its value to sink, making British goods cheaper abroad and boosting exports while shrinking imports. Some even accused the Bank of England of selling sterling to push the pound lower! Others believed that a massive switch of funds from pounds to another currency was the cause and that the Bank of England could not counter the selling. Whatever the reason, the pound continued to slide over the next few weeks, producing new strains on the floating system. As a result, funds were moved around during this period to avoid what were considered weak currencies, such as the French franc, even though no crisis was attached directly to them, and finding haven in stronger currencies, such as the West German mark or Swiss franc. This put even greater strains on the European joint float, which France left in March.

The major concerns with these developments were (1) that Italy and Britain were gaining trade advantages at other nations' expense as their currencies declined; (2) that the "managed" float wasn't really that manageable and currency stability was not an achievable goal; (3) that the new spirit of economic cooperation and agreement reached at Rambouillet and Jamaica was not strong enough to withstand crisis.

If these concerns proved to be valid, then indeed

a dismal outlook for monetary affairs was ahead. On the other hand, some felt that basic underlying economic fundamentals were the real cause of the pound and lira crises and that once they worked themselves out, floating would be calmer in the future.

Dorado Beach, Puerto Rico:
A Long Way From Rambouillet?

In light of the growing concern with these monetary developments, the world leaders decided to meet again and hold another economic summit, this time for two days in Puerto Rico in June, 1976. In attendance were President Ford, British Prime Minister James Callaghan, West German Chancellor Helmut Schmidt, Japanese Prime Minister Takeo Miki, French President Valery Giscard d' Estaing, Italian Premier Aldo Moro and Canadian Prime Minister Pierre Trudeau. Their agenda concerned mutual economic issues, and included the progress of the stalled trade talks in Geneva, the pace of Western economic recovery from the recession, concern about the renewal of inflation, aid for developing nations, raw material agreements with Third World nations and recent currency developments. After two days of meetings, the Summit produced only one surprise: a proposal to use an old accord, the General Arrangement to Borrow, established in 1962 by the Group of 10 industrial nations, to help nations currently experiencing major balance of payment problems, like Italy. No specifics of this proposal were announced. But as expected, the conference produced Rambouillet-type statements, emphasizing the continuation of moderate economic policies to recover from the recession and avoid inflation. On the monetary side, it was again emphasized that nations should avoid protectionist currency manipulations. The possibility of another economic summit later in Tokyo was also mentioned. In many respects, this follow-up to Rambouillet was a copy of Rambouillet.

Manila Prelude: Currency Turmoil

In the autumn of 1976, not only did the leaves begin to fall, so did some major currencies. In early September, the Mexican government ended 22 years of fixed parity for the peso and let it float against other currencies. The peso was one of the last major currencies still not floating. For some time, given the inflation and other economic problems in Mexico, many expected the devaluation and floating of the peso but this was consistently denied by the Mexican government. But it did happen and the peso dropped almost 40% in value. The government said that this move was temporary and that it would re-establish parity for the peso sometime in the future. But the time was not specified.

An even greater crisis occurred late in September, just one week before the IMF annual meeting in Manila and involved the British pound. The pound began to take "a pounding" in the currency markets and declined in value to an all-time low of just under $1.64. The continuing economic, labor, political, and even weather problems in England were the most frequently given explanations for the precipitous drop. The pound's plunge created a monetary crisis as well and the Labor government of James Callaghan turned to the IMF for a $3.9 billion loan to help it through this period of monetary turmoil. The pound stabilized as news of this action was released. But this recent pound crisis raised further doubts about the soundness of the pound. To many, it also emphasized the importance of the underlying domestic economy as the major determinant of a nation's currency value.

The Manila IMF

The 1976 annual meeting of the IMF and World Bank opened in Manila one week later, in early October. It was anticipated that the British request for an IMF loan of $3.9 billion would be discussed in Manila. It was also expected that the controversial IMF gold sales (see Chapter IV) would be on the agenda. Beyond these contemporary problems, the Manila meeting was not expected to generate any major change in the structure of the world monetary system.

As it turned out, the joint IMF-World Bank annual meeting had more of a banking emphasis than a strictly currency one. As expected, England began preliminary negotiations with the IMF for its loan. While the IMF could supply a multibillion-dollar loan, it was also possible that part of the loan would come through the General Arrangement to Borrow. The GAB had been established in 1962 by the Group of 10 and recently resurrected at the Puerto Rican meeting as a potential source of assistance for Italy. A decision on the loan request of England was scheduled for November or December.

Banking concerns were also evident in other discussions, especially those related to the growing problem of needy nations getting financial assistance from private sources. In general, bankers were critical of nations (a) seeking outside help rather than taking the necessary hard steps to solve their basic economic problems; (b) turning to private banks and markets for Eurocurrency-type loans instead of going to international agencies such as the IMF or World Bank.

In terms of currency matters, very little was expected from this IMF meeting and little happened. While the IMF awaited the approval of the proposed change in its charter to legalize the floating not much could be done. On the gold front, the IMF was determined to go ahead with its scheduled gold auctions, despite the complaints of the Common Market and South Africa.

Manila Postlude

As was pointed out in an editorial which appeared in the *Journal* just a few days after the conclusion of the IMF meeting in Manila, it was "no thrilla." But some thrills and excitement in the form of monetary turmoil soon appeared involving the British pound, the Canadian dollar, the Mexican peso, and the West German mark. The pattern was similar to what had happened after the Jamaica IMF Committee meetings of January, 1976: a currency crisis on the heels of surface calm during an official meeting. The irony of the situation was that as the IMF finally settled down and awaited the legitimization of the floating system, that system once again became volatile.

The West German mark was the first source of excitement. Long considered the strongest member of the snake, the mark had repeatedly withstood upward pressure to revalue. As late as a few days before the revaluation took place, official reports from West Germany continued to deny that it was going to happen. But on Sunday, October 19, to the surprise of many, the snake was realigned internally with the mark rising 2% against the Dutch guilder and the Belgian and Luxembourg francs, 3% against the Swedish krona and the Norwegian krone and 6% against the Danish krone. The immediate reaction by currency dealers was that the revaluation did not go far enough and that the mark was still undervalued. Thus, another revaluation was expected and upward pressure on the mark resumed.

The problems within the snake led to some reconsideration of adopting a "crawling peg" system. This system would provide a way of avoiding the buildup of pressure on a currency by making frequent small adjustments to its official value. The crawling peg system was a compromise between the floating and fixed—a currency value is fixed, but revised frequently. The hope is that frequent and small changes in the value of the currency will eliminate pressures that build up over time and require major changes which are less attractive to monetary leaders.

Next, a major crisis again developed for the British pound, which hit a new low on October 26 of $1.5750. The immediate trigger was a report in the British press that the IMF and the U.S. had agreed that a lower value for the pound (around $1.50) was a condition for the $3.9 billion loan sought by Britain. The report was, of course, denied but the pound continued to be shaky. Three other factors contributed to a general lack of confidence in the pound: the high level of government spending in the British economy, the high level of British inflation and the large amount of foreign owned sterling balances which were volatile during any crisis. During this period of genuine crisis in the pound, the confidence level sank so low as to prompt talk of the "British ounce."

The overall atmosphere was further unsettled by a second devaluation of the Mexican peso in late October. After 22 years of fixed value (12.5 pesos equal $1.00) the peso was devalued 40% in late August against the dollar and allowed to float; then in September the peso again was fixed in value against the dollar (19.7 to $1.00). But due to what was called a capital flight, the new fixed rate was abandoned on October 28 and the peso immediately lost another 25%. Now the American dollar bought more than 26 pesos, twice the number that it did before the first devaluation just two months earlier. The official explanation was that the first devaluation caused Mexican citizens to lose confidence in the peso and convert their pesos into stronger currencies thereby putting downward pressure on the peso. One day after the second devaluation, the IMF announced that it was assembling an aid program totaling $963 million to assist the Mexican economy and this bolstered confidence in the peso for a time.

However, the peso's problems returned in November and resulted in a third devaluation of the peso on November 22 when the Mexican central bank withdrew its support of the peso. It then dropped to a new low value of 3.5 U.S. cents.

The three peso devaluations cut the number of Mexicans touring abroad and affected American-Mexican business relations close to the American border. There is considerable American-Mexican business along the border and the three devaluations had opposing affects on the profitability of Mexican operations for American firms: the dollar cost of Mexican labor and material was lowered, but the dollar value of Mexican sales and revenues was reduced as well.

The pound crisis continued for about a week with widespread consequences. It contributed to renewed upward pressure on the West German mark as money fled from the pound into the mark. It raised questions about Britain's ability to continue to support NATO commitments, as Britain looked for ways to help its balance of payments. And the political unity in the Common Market was strained by the pound crisis and mark revaluation. In the currency markets, the possibility of a $1.50 pound loomed as a reality. But after a week of turmoil, the pound settled down in early November at values in the low $1.60s.

In late October, another cloud appeared on the

horizon: the scheduled meeting of the OPEC ministers in mid-December at Doha, Qatar to consider another rise in the price of oil, with all that might bring.

At that meeting, a pricing disagreement developed and it was resolved by a split level price increase for the first six months of 1977. Saudi Arabia and the Arab Emirates decided to increase the price of their oil by 5%, whereas the rest of OPEC would increase their price by 10%. The world was surprised by this split in OPEC but by the end of 1976, the implications of this were not yet clear.

It is also important to note another event in early November, 1976 which may have quite an impact on currency values for a time to come—the election of Jimmy Carter as President of the U.S. and the change in the administration in Washington. The immediate result on both the U.S. dollar and the Dow Jones Index in the New York Stock Exchange was negative. Correspondingly, the price of gold rose. On these markets, uncertainty over Mr. Carter and his policies was the main cause and this was expected. President-elect Carter's immediate attention was focused on domestic economic issues and problems and restructuring the federal government. But he did agree to attend a Rambouillet-type, top level economic summit (called the Downing Street Summit) in May, 1977, in London to discuss international economic and monetary issues with the leaders of Great Britain, France, Italy, West Germany, Canada, and Japan.

Throughout most of 1976, the Canadian dollar was higher than the U.S. dollar. But this ended in November. The Parti Quebecois was elected to power in Quebec Province on November 15. Concerns about the separatist policies of the party and some questions about the overall health of the Canadian economy were seen as the reasons behind the decline of the

Canadian dollar below parity with the U.S. dollar, which happened in late November.

The year ended with some good news and some bad news for Britain. The good news prevailed and the pound ended the year on a strong note. The bad news came in mid-December as the Labor Party announced a package of tax increases and government spending cuts. These were seen as a condition for getting the $3.9 billion IMF loan that Britain wanted. This package was given a favorable nod less than a week later by the members of the balance of payments panel of the OECD who were reviewing the IMF loan request. One day later, the Group of 10 announced a decision to lend Britain approximately $3 billion through the IMF under the 1962 General Arrangement to Borrow pact. And within 10 days, the good news: Britain received approval from the IMF for the $3.9 billion loan.

Assessing Dashed Hopes

This recent period of meetings and economic summits points out how limited the policies, plans, and objectives set by monetary negotiations are in controlling currency markets. For the world of monetary affairs and indeed in a broader sense, for the world as a whole, the 1970s may well be remembered as the time when major world-wide economic and political problems could not be resolved quickly by political negotiation or agreement. The monetary meetings, as far back as Nairobi, held out hope for progress and cooperation and produced optimism. But subsequent events contradicted that optimism and many found themselves disappointed and disillusioned. Perhaps a realistic attitude is somewhere between high optimism about the effectiveness of economic summits and IMF meetings and complete pessimism and skepticism toward such meetings. Recent history indicates that there is a limit on what can be accomplished through international accord and this had best be recognized in advance.

PS: Whither Floated the Dollar?

This chapter has covered one of the most dynamic and uncertain periods in the history of international monetary affairs: the floating of February 1973 to December, 1976. During this period, attention has focused on various currencies and SDRs and on related economic topics such as energy, inflation, recession, and aid for developing nations. Of natural concern is how the dollar did during this period. That is, what was the dollar's value in general compared to all currencies and then how the dollar did against specific currencies. Appendix A presents the value, in dollars, of the world's major currencies and gold for the period of January, 1972 through December, 1976, based on the selling prices of bank transfers in the U.S. for payment abroad for the currencies. An examination of it will show in detail how each currency moved relative to the dollar. In general, the movement of the dollar during this critical floating period can be seen in the following highlights:

(1) Early 1974: the dollar was making a comeback from the decline of early 1973 when the dollar underwent its second devaluation. By early 1974 the dollar was generally rising in value, largely due to a degree of independence from outside oil compared with other industrial nations.

(2) Early 1975: the dollar was generally declining, a result of American inflation in 1974 and the business downturn which affected the U.S. before it did other nations.

(3) Late 1975: by September, 1975, the dollar was again improving: 3.8% higher than after the second devaluation in February, 1973.

(4) Early 1976: The Morgan Guaranty Trust Company in New York has prepared an index of the dollar's value, adjusted for trade significance, against 14 other currencies and this is regularly published in the *Journal*. On this basis, the January 2, 1976 dollar was 4.04% higher than after the second devaluation in February, 1973 but down 1.79% from the value at December, 1971 and down 12.3% from the value at June, 1970. Comparing 14 currencies for the period June 1970 to December, 1975, trade-adjusted, the changes in currency values as prepared by Morgan Guaranty and published in the January 2, 1976 *Journal*, were:

Swiss franc	+35.08%
West German mark	+17.97
Japanese yen	+10.73
Canadian dollar	+ 4.16
French franc	+ 3.98
British pound	−36.76
U.S. dollar	−12.31
Italian lira	−31.87

(5) End of 1976: the dollar was at its highest value in the past four years, as measured by the Morgan Guaranty figures. On December 1, 1976, the dollar opened 6.42% higher than after February, 1973 and .35% above the rate prevailing after the December, 1971 devaluation.

Taking specific currencies mentioned in this chapter and looking at Appendix A, this is how they did against the dollar during the period of February, 1973 to December, 1976:

(1) The Swiss franc: overall, the Swiss franc rose in value against the dollar during this period although there were times of increases and later reversals.

(2) British pound: the dollar generally rose in value against the pound, especially in the period of July, 1975 to November, 1976 when the pound dropped fast.

(3) West German mark: the mark generally rose during the period, but the dollar gained slightly against the mark during the period of July, 1975 to June, 1976. From June, 1976 until the end of the year, the mark rose.

(4) French franc: the franc was very uneven against the dollar, but stable overall. In early 1975 the dollar lost against the franc but in the period of November, 1975 to December, 1976, the franc dropped.

(5) Japanese yen: the dollar rose against the yen in 1974 and 1975, but the yen came back against the dollar in 1976. However, at the end of 1976, the yen began to drop.

Fundamentals
Of Currency Valuation

These statistics lead to consideration of what affects the value of a currency. This topic has been touched upon in previous sections but of concern here is the period of February, 1973 to December, 1976 during the float. The lack of any plan for a return to fixed exchange rates, and new economic relationships created by the energy crisis, the new economic-political conccsciousness of the Third World nations, and efforts at the establishment of basic commodity pacts have altered significantly previous analyses of currency values. The following factors have strongly influenced the value of the floating currencies, and with the floating expected to continue, they will be the factors to watch in determining future values:

(1) The total demand and supply of a given currency, an in particular the components of supply and demand for that currency as detailed here.

(2) The speed of recovery from a recession, relative to other nations. This was a very important factor in 1975-76.

(3) A nation's vulnerability to energy embargoes, critical in 1974.

(4) A nation's trade and payment balances.

(5) The supply of a given currency as determined by domestic monetary policy and the relative growth in the domestic money supply.

(6) Stability at the national economy, including inflation rate, political stability, national prosperity, labor costs, and unemployment rates.

(7) A currency's vulnerability to rumors. Strong currencies tend to get stronger and weak currencies weaker.

(8) Domestic interest rates and changes in these rates. If interest rates are relatively high, others will want to obtain that currency and invest it in the securities of that nation and earn high yields.

(9) The strength or weakness of domestic GNP as a major gauge of a nation's underlying economic strength.

(10) Confidence and expectations, especially during uncertainty and crisis.

(11) In a dirty float, the amount of governmental intervention.

While it is not very difficult to identify and list the factors, of critical importance is determining the relative weight of each in explaining cause and effect relationships and in predicting future values. All of this is a world away from the relative certainty of a fixed rate system.

Chapter III

Fixed & Floating: Friends and Foes

Basic Nature
Of Monetary Affairs:
Ripe for Debate

An often unrecognized aspect of international monetary affairs is its classification as an art rather than as a science. An art is defined as a nonscientific branch of learning. Thus, issues in international monetary affairs cannot be resolved by reference to natural laws or laboratory experiments. Victories in international monetary debates are won by reason, thought, and what seems to work or work best and this is indeed fertile field for natural disagreement among the experts. In recent times, given the collapse of the Bretton Woods and Smithsonian agreements and their replacement with an "interim" system of floating rates, few issues in monetary affairs have generated as much debate as fixed vs. floating exchange rates.

The following readings present the differing opinions of monetary authorities on fixed vs. floating rates and describe the relevant issues in this debate. The authors have different backgrounds and viewpoints, although writing as individuals, collectively they provide a broad view into contemporary monetary thinking. As will become evident, much of the debate centered on the effect of fixed vs. floating rates on national economies and on international trade and payment balances. The views of Professor Laffer presented in Reading 2, Chapter I, sparked considerable controversy and debate and Reading 2 may be read in conjunction with the following readings.

READING 7

The Case for Fixed Exchange Rates

JUDE WANNISKI

When economic policymakers get together in Washington they fret that the usual economic medicine no longer seems to work—inflation seems oblivious to fiscal discipline, tighter money, dampened demand or increased supply, or even new proposals to tie the economy to the consumer price index. But at least, the policymakers sigh, our international problems have been solved by floating exchange rates.

There are, though, at least two economists who are prepared to argue that floating exchange rates are precisely the reason the rest of the medicine no longer works. Arthur B. Laffer and Robert Mundell are proponents of an unorthodox view of international economics. They believe that the fundamental cause of the current world inflation is excess growth in the world money supply, but that floating rates are a structural cause that "ratchets" the inflation into double-digit figures. And they believe the world cannot solve the inflation until it arranges a system of truly fixed exchange rates.

After all, Professors Mundell and Laffer

point out, the moderate inflation of the 1950s and 1960s ended in 1968, when exchange-rate changes began taking place with some frequency. Inflation speeded further after August 1971, when exchange-rate changes were taking place with rapidity. And when fixity was abandoned and the world began floating in February last year, the world became wildly inflationary.

The Mundell-Laffer Argument

In the Mundell-Laffer view of the world economy, this result is inevitable. Their theoretical model rests on a basic assumption they argue is a close approximation of reality in today's increasingly integrated economic world. This is that an article's real price—that is, its value relative to other articles rather than to national currencies—cannot be different in two nations with closely related economies. If it were, supplies of that article would simply flow from one nation to another until the real prices were equal.

If this is true, it follows that when one country devalues its currency in relation to another country, prices as measured by the two currencies will adjust to compensate for the change; the nominal prices will change to maintain equal real prices. And from this seemingly simple proposition flow a number of unorthodox conclusions.

One, for example, is that a nation cannot improve its balance of trade by devaluing; it will achieve no competitive advantage because nominal prices will change and real prices will not. A second is that a nation that does devalue its currency will suffer extraordinary inflation; if real prices remain unchanged, its nominal prices will have to go up faster than the rest of the world's.

In a world of constantly floating exchange rates one more factor becomes important: Prices are rigid in the downward direction. That is, prices move up more easily than they move down. If there were no rigidities and country A devalued against country B, half of the adjustment would show up as higher nominal prices in country A, and half as lower nominal prices in country B. But because of the downward rigidity, a disproportionate amount of the adjustment takes the form of inflation in the devaluing country.

So suppose that floating exchange rates prevailed between currency A, perhaps the dollar, and currency B, perhaps a bundle of European currencies. And suppose A depreciates by 10% on six months, and appreciates by the same amount in the next six months. Nominal prices in both countries adjust to compensate for these changes in exchange rates. In the first six months a disproportionate share of the adjustment takes place through inflation in nation A, and in the second six a disproportionate share takes place through inflation in nation B. Thus at the end of the year the exchange rates are unchanged, but nominal prices in both nations are higher. The float has ratcheted world inflation to a higher level.

The view that floating exchange rates foster inflation is only one part of a far larger economic viewpoint Professors Laffer and Mundell have been developing. They argue strongly for fixed exchange rates, as a method of promoting world economic integration. And while most proponents of fixed rates are traditional economists forever constructing elaborate mechanisms trying to approximate the 19th Century gold standard, these two professors argue from a monetarist economic viewpoint, usually associated with floating rates.

Professor Mundell, a 41-year-old Canadian renowned in the profession for his brilliance— he picked up his Ph.D. in six months' residency at MIT 18 years ago—was the prime mover in conceptualizing the theory. Professor Laffer, 33—on the faculty of Chicago's Graduate School of Business at 27—has been the more flamboyant and aggressive of the two, both in working through the rigorous underpinnings of the theory and in presenting it. They were drawn together at Chicago six years ago and began applying the Friedman monetarist model of the U.S. economy to the world.

Their sharp differences with Professor Friedman on the exchange-rate issue is the result of this difference in perspective.

The typical monetarist argument for floating exchange rates holds that only through pure floating can a country gain independence over its monetary policy. When central banks are not required by agreement to intervene in order to support a "weak" currency, the country whose currency is weak is forced to accept the consequences of the easy-money policies that made the currency weak. It will no longer be able to "export" inflation, and by the same token it will not have to import the inflation caused by excess money creation outside its borders. Floating advocates say this is desirable, that it exerts an internal discipline on each monetary authority to act responsibly.

Professors Laffer and Mundell agree that floating rates give each nation independence in monetary policy, but they believe such independence is undesirable. It interferes with maximum economic efficiency, in effect serving as an economic barrier such as tariffs or quotas.

In viewing the world itself as a closed economic system, they say it is recognized as being desirable that there be one price for wheat and zero barriers to trade, thereby assuring that wheat will be produced by the most efficient. So, too, in a closed national economy, or in an ideal integrated world economy, there would be one money, a common currency in which all prices are measured and all transactions take place. In a less than ideal world, this condition can be approximated by truly and absolutely fixed exchange rates. If rates are fixed, devaluation and revaluations of money no longer interfere with the efficiencies of a free market.

The idea that a fixed system is a market system and a floating system a controlled one is the most difficult Mundell-Laffer concept to see. Its essence is that when rates float, the central bank of each country has a monopoly over its money supply; when rates are fixed, the citizens of the participant countries share in a common money pool with no interference by their respective governments.

Under a float, the citizens of the United States, in order to satisfy their money demands, have to rely exclusively on the individuals who run the Federal Reserve to produce the precise money supply to meet demand. Because the individuals at the Fed can never know precisely what the demand is, they can only make rough guesses, and are always wrong in one direction or the other. If an excess is produced at a given instant in time, it cannot be exported for use by other countries. If a shortfall is produced, U.S. citizens cannot make up the difference by borrowing foreign currency and converting it to dollars.

Under a fixed-rate system, by contrast, the central banks of the system do not have to be precise in their production of money. If they produce too much, foreigners will borrow it, take it to their central banks, and convert it to local currencies. If the Fed produces too little at a given instant, money demanders here will borrow abroad and convert those foreign currencies to dollars by presenting them at a central bank.

Under fixed rates, inflation will still result if the world money supply—the aggregate of the money created by all the central banks—grows faster than productive resources. But because the money is shared, the inflation rate will be similar in all countries. And of course, the inflation caused to excessive money growth will not be intensified by the ratcheting effect of floating rates with downward price rigidity.

Beyond that, because the integrating effect of a common money promotes total economic efficiency, there are conditions in which it can combat both inflation and unemployment simultaneously. To explain this, Professors Laffer and Mundell use a simplified two-country model. Consider country A, which uses dollars and has a 10% inflation rate and 0% unemployment. Country B uses francs, has a 0% inflation rate and 10% unemployment. Country A clearly has too few goods and no more workers; country B has all the goods it needs and too many workers. Given independent money systems, country A can't make use of the surplus workers in country B; country B can't make use of the surplus money of country A to employ its workers. Given a common currency or a fixed exchange-rate system, the transfer is made and both countries have no inflation and no unemployment.

Fixing exchange rates, in the Mundell-Laffer view, would not cure inflation. But it would reduce it by removing the ratcheting effect, and would provide a structure under which the central banks could coordinate their money-creation policies in a way that would control the remaining inflation.

Their proposals for how to fix rates are simple in the economic sense. At least one major country, the U.S. being the best candidate, would have to accept the discipline of primary reserve or asset convertibility, while other currencies were kept convertible into that major intervention currency at fixed rates. Governments would be obligated to sell unlimited quantities of their currency at the floor price, and would borrow whatever reserves would be needed to fight speculative runs.

The U.S. would manage its money supply using world money growth as a target, keeping this at an appropriate level by compensating for money creation of other central banks. The Mundell-Laffer model assumes that any such system would involve multinational policy review. Governments that needed to borrow foreign exchange from other governments would pay market rates of interest, which would be an important element of discipline in the system.

This system would break down, as other fixed rate systems have in the past, if one of the governments inflated its money supply to the point where it runs out of reserve assets and cannot borrow more. At that point, a government will devalue its currency, hoping to improve its competitiveness vis-a-vis its trading partners. The payment of market interest rates on borrowed reserves is intended to persuade governments that are inflating faster than others that it would be cheaper to get their money growth in line.

The political problem, of course, is to persuade governments to give up the option of inflating their currencies and devaluing. Professors Laffer and Mundell are more optimistic on this score than most observers, simply because their economic view tells them this option does not work anyway, and because governments seem to be learning the same thing through experience.

The experience of recent years, after all, has been that inflating currencies does not cure unemployment. Since the days of the Smithsonian Agreement, governments seem to be learning that devaluation doesn't help a country's trade position and revaluation doesn't hurt it. Floating exchange rates have certainly coincided with abnormally high inflation.

None of this experience conforms to usual economic models, but it conforms perfectly with the Mundell-Laffer one. And if governments came to believe that the latter model describes their economic problems, their political problems would no longer look so insurmountable.

READING 8

In Defense of Floating Rates

DAVID I. MEISELMAN

Claiming that the old medicine no longer works to diagnose or to cure inflation, an article in The Wall Street Journal referred the patient to Professors Arthur B. Laffer and Robert Mundell. They claim that the 1973 inflation in the United States was much greater than the old theories would have predicted because of foreign exchange devaluation of the U.S. dollar and the widespread adoption of floating rates, both of which occurred early in 1973.

Aside from the embarrassing fact that U.S. inflation accelerated during the second half of the year while the dollar appreciated, it turns out that the 1973 inflation can better be explained by existing analysis. Their exercise may well be another example of new theories being spun to explain non-existent facts.

An alternative explanation of recent inflation draws on the single most tested set of propositions in all of economics which has explained every important change in the level of prices which has been studied for at least 400 years. This view asserts that inflation results when the quantity of money increases faster than output, that deflation occurs when money declines relative to output, and that the price level tends to be stable when the ratio of money to output is stable. Since the 1930s in the United States and throughout the rest of the world, money has increased more rapidly than output, causing a long era of almost continuous world-wide inflation.

The accompanying chart shows the close connections since 1960 between the rising ratio of money to output and the resulting rising level of prices for the U.S. The chart was

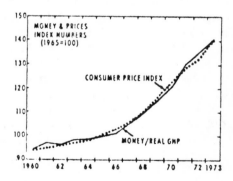

taken from a study of the current inflation I presented at the recently held Conference on World-Wide Inflation sponsored by The American Enterprise Institute. It shows that the burst of inflation since 1973 has followed historic norms of economic behavior. This chart uses the broad M-2 measure of money that includes currency plus all commercial bank deposits other than large certificates of deposit. The same close relationship holds for the narrow M-1 measure of currency plus demand deposits when adjusted for secular drift in the ratio of 2.7% per year.

Inflation abroad also fits the same pattern and is documented in the study.

The world-wide acceleration of inflation since 1973 resulted primarily from a speedup in the pace of monetary expansion throughout the world rather than from declines in output stemming from such oft-cited events as the disappearance of anchovies off the coast of Peru or the operations of the OPEC oil cartel. To be sure, there was some reduction in the output of petroleum and chicken feed, which explains why these prices increased relative to other prices. Also, real GNP fell in the first quarter of 1974. But aggregate output in the United States and throughout the world is now higher than it was in early 1973 despite isolated examples of reductions in supplies of a handful of products. Thus the increase in the ratio of money to output has been the result of sharp increases in money rather than decreases in output. In the U.S., since 1971 both the narrow M-1 and the broad M-2 measures of money have been rising at the fastest rates since World War II. Not surprisingly, prices have also been rising at the fastest pace since 1946. Since Federal Reserve actions determined the quantity of money, the Fed rather than the fish in Peru is primarily to blame for our inflation woes.

Freed from foreign constraints by the

1968 two-tier gold arrangement and the 1972 closing of the gold window, the Fed has erred on the side of excessive monetary ease ever since.

A Staggering Increase

For the nine major OECD advanced economies I have surveyed, which include Canada, Germany, Japan and Great Britain, over the three years of 1971 through 1973 the nominal quantity of money increased a staggering 56%, mainly as a direct result of their last ditch efforts to retard appreciation of their own exchange rates (the depreciation of the U.S. dollar) and to prevent the collapse of the Bretton Woods pseudo-fixed exchange rates system. They failed at both. To prevent the rise in the price of their own currencies relative to the dollar, foreign central banks purchased a huge volume of U.S. dollars, which they financed by merely creating a huge volume of new money. Large German and Japanese surpluses required large-scale expansion of the volume of Deutschemarks and yen.

The episode was another illustration of the general proposition that countries with fixed exchange rates cannot effectively determine their own money supplies and thereby their price levels. The quantity of money typically becomes a by-product of the balance of payments, a small tail indeed to be wagging a large dog, especially for countries such as the United States where exports and imports are each only a small 8% of GNP. Through these and related mechanisms, the fixed rate system in recent years had become an engine of inflation, especially since deficiet countries never effectively deflated, partly because they were able to borrow newly created reserves from the International Monetary Fund. In other eras, such as during the world-wide economic collapse of the early 1930s, adherence to the fixed rates caused deflation by requiring monetary contraction by deficit countries. Deflation appears to have been ruled out by world-wide adherence to full employment policies which conflict with the tendency for monetary restriction to lead first to reductions in employment and output before later price reductions.

It was not until fixed rates and heavy central bank intervention were abandoned early in 1973 that these countries could gain control over their money. The subsequent events hold out promise for a slowing of inflation outside the U.S., but do not guarantee it. As we have seen, U.S. monetary independence has been used to hasten rather than slow inflation. The average annual rate of monetary expansion of 26% in the fourth quarter of 1972 was brought down to 5% by the fourth quarter of 1973. Countries such as Germany and Holland were actually able to reduce their money stocks, at least temporarily.

The system of freely floating rates is a free market in foreign exchange with the well known merits of other free markets, but with the added virtue that it breaks the link between the balance of payments and the stock of money. Under floating rates there is no central bank price fixing or other intervention in foreign exchange markets, no balance of payments surpluses and deficits and thereby no need for central banks to increase money in response to surpluses or to reduce money in response to deficits. Inflation abroad need not be imported, nor can inflation-creating money be exported if other countries are unwilling to monetize balance of payments deficits.

Only under floating rates can countries pursue independent monetary policies, including those leading to generally stable price levels. Proposals to use fiscal policy, tax and government expenditures tools under fixed rates to achieve internal stability and external balance are deficient because they lack long-term effects and their short-run impacts are either too undependable or too weak. Proposals for direct controls over capital movements or trade are essentially disguised devaluations with many undesirable side effects which impair personal freedom and reduce economic efficiency. Moreover, under fixed rates disturbances from abroad tend to be magnified rather than buffered, in part because they are generally amplified by the link to domestic money.

Proposals for fixed rates, even when rates are adjustable from time to time, require central bank intervention whenever rates move beyond some predetermined range, and there is no way to estimate the monetary consequences of alternative pegged rates. These arrangements have the serious deficiency that they weaken monetary control. In some countries central banks can engage in operations to offset unwanted changes in bank reserves. However, the record is clear that central banks are reluctant to do so, even in the few countries such as the United States and the United Kingdom which have the highly developed capital markets able to absorb large scale open market operations.

Messrs. Laffer and Mundell, in contrast with this view, believe that the world-wide speedup of inflation since early 1973 is the direct result of the foreign exchange devaluation of the U.S. dollar and of the general abandonment of fixed rates. They argue that devaluations raise the prices of imports and exports, which is correct, that prices of individual products are flexible upward (correct) but not downward (incorrect, witness the more than 50% fall of the prices of wool, soybean meal and bacon in the past year of inflation or the large number of declining retail and wholesale prices when the price index approached stability in the late 1950s and early 1960s). Messrs. Laffer and Mundell thereby claim that devaluation causes price increases in the depreciating countries, but that there are no corresponding price declines in appreciating countries. Even in the world of stable but not rigidly fixed rates, random fluctuations would cause a ratcheting up of prices for each short-lived exchange rate movement.

The Laffer-Mundell Conclusion

Becaue they believe that devaluation does not alter either the trade balance or the terms of trade, they conclude that the volume of goods is unaffected by devaluation. Thereby, devaluation has no effect on the balance of payments which might induce changes in the stock of money, even under the central bank intervention required by fixed exchange rates.

Since, in the Laffer-Mundell theory, neither output nor money is altered by devaluation, there is no effective mechanism to create inflation.

My own view is that devaluation does have a relatively small inflationary impact because devaluation does tend to worsen the terms of trade. Since we must deliver more exports to pay for the same imports, devaluation results in a decline in aggregate productivity and output. For a given money stock, prices are correspondingly higher.

My colleague Wilson Schmidt made some rough calculations along these lines and found that between 1971 and 1973 the U.S. terms of trade worsened by 5.6%. But given the small weight of international trade in our GNP of about 8%, the worsened terms of trade led to a less than one-half of 1% reduction in real GNP (5.6% of the 8%) with the price index equivalently no more than 0.5% higher at the end of 1973. Over the same period the consumer price index increased a total of 10% and the wholesale price index rose 19%. U.S. inflation must therefore be labelled "Made in the U.S." rather than "Imported."

Finally, Messrs. Laffer and Mundell have proposed a new international monetary system based on fixed exchange rates in which the U.S. is the world's central bank, maintaining dollar convertibility at fixed rates and managing the U.S. money stock in order to achieve a stable world price level.

Even if a single world price index were a meaningful measure, given the vast international differences in incomes, consumption standards and tastes, there are insurmountable problems reconciling differences among foreign nations and coordinating their monetary policies. European Common Market countries, with far closer economic and political ties than typically found elsewhere in the world, have some successful experience in coordinating other economic policies, but have never been able to approach coordination of their separate monetary policies.

For post-Vietnam United States there are special hazards and dubious rewards to be derived from a special role as the world's monetary policeman, including the necessity to enforce rules of the fixed rate system of deficit countries, most of whom would regard the required deflation and economic slowdown as excessively harsh and unacceptable means to achieve balance of payments equilibrium. Conflicts with domestic policies and the diffusion of world economic and political power make it unlikely that the U.S. or any other country can ever be the 20th Century counterpart of the 19th Century Bank of England.

In addition, the Laffer-Mundell proposal has strong inflationary biases. To become the world's central bank and maintain convertibility, the U.S. must effectively go through a large devaluation in order to accumulate the necessary foreign exchange to ensure the viability and credibility of the system. By their own analysis, the devaluation would lead to more U.S. inflation as we traded goods for foreign exchange. The alternative route is the current exchange rate but with unilateral U.S. monetary restriction and deflation. Neither would seem to be acceptable.

A return to fixed rates would renew the series of periodic speculative runs against world currencies which played an important role in the inflationary increase in the world money supply in the decade before the demise of the fixed rate system in 1973. Surplus countries would again be required to monetize speculative inflows to prevent appreciation and deficit countries would again beg and borrow newly created reserves to prevent or forestall devaluation.

READING 9

A Route to Monetary Discipline

WILLIAM C. CATES

Without doubt there is no economic conundrum today as complex and perplexing as is the question of gold and the international monetary system. In our bewilderment we leave this arcane subject to Treasury "experts" or to "gold bugs" here and abroad, with few in between having the temerity to raise it for public discussion. Yet the international monetary system will either be the rock upon which Western civilization stands or the sand over which it crumbles. Destroy the currency and you destroy the kingdom.

The immediate issues, which will probably be left unresolved by the June, 1975 negotiations among 126 member nations of the International Monetary Fund, are code words for reality: 1. Should "normal" behavior consist of floating or fixed exchange rates? (We favor floating, the French, fixing.) 2. Should U.S. voting rights in the IMF fall below the limited veto powers provided by 20%? 3. Should central banks be permitted to buy as well as sell gold? (French position: yes; American: no.)

In the years immediately preceding the closing of the gold window on August 15, 1971, the Treasury Department saw the United States as a Gulliver, its dollar strapped down by the Lilliputian strings of European and Japanese fixed currency parities. In the Treasury view the exchange rates of these other countries were pegged at such low levels as to erode the United States position in world trade—to the benefit of Europe and Japan—as well as to drain gold reserves from U.S. vaults.

Years of argument, statistical demonstration, cajolery and browbeating failed to budge other nations from their artificially low exchange parities. The dollar was the "heavy" currency against which all others were free to peg at whatever price seemed to bring the maximum advantage in trade and payments. Even after we closed the gold window and imposed a 10% temporary import surcharge to make the dollar dilemma clear, the December 1971 negotiations at the Smithsonian Institution to fix more realistic exchange rates resembled bargaining in a Turkish bazaar. As events have shown, the new parities that other nations were willing to concede were far from sufficient to "clear the market" and restore equilibrium to world trade and payments.

Nightmares at Treasury

Small wonder that the Treasury shies away from fixed exchange rates. Their restoration could again leave the United States helpless against artificial exchange pegging by other nations, particularly if we must undertake to "defend" the dollar against all comers by selling what is left of our gold reserves and-or going into debt to the IMF. The nightmare from which responsible Treasury officials awoke in increasingly cold sweats as the Sixties wore on culminated with a vision of themselves humbly submitting the federal budget to the supercilious scrutiny of our creditors: European finance ministers and bureaucrats from the IMF. There is a fine line between prudence and paranoia, and perhaps like most nightmares this one looks silly in the daylight. But a return to fixed exchange rates will probably have to be evolutionary and experimental, to guard against a global raid on United States reserves.

The newly-minted congressional monetarists think they're onto a good thing, to wit, political control of the nation's money supply in order to gain full employment, low interest rates, and re-election. With such noble goals at stake they are determined to make sure that U.S. officials do not, in some international arena, bargain away our monetary independence. Alas, in monetary policy as elsewhere, a little knowledge is a dangerous thing. Congress has learned that the economy can be manipulated by changing the money supply; it has not learned what monetarists from Milton Friedman on down have been shouting into deaf ears for decades: don't mess with the money supply!

Specifically "messing" means that if the nation's money supply is increased at a rate which exceeds the real output of goods and services, not only will inflation be the result but by now an entire populace, tuned like a fiddle string to inflation's prospect, will try to discount it through borrowing, and interest rates will *rise*. Looking back over the past decade one can see that each increase in the money supply above and beyond the growth of real Gross National Product has rapidly resulted in higher rather than lower interest rates. Furthermore, the money market reaction to such monetary manipulation is becoming increasingly sensitive: in the past 18 months even short-term interest rates in the United States have correlated remarkably and in the same direction with money supply changes.

In short we have reached the point where fiddling with the money supply will no longer fool the public. No sovereign can successfully clip coins if the town crier stands with a pair of scales beneath the palace window. Congress must rid itself of the notion that coin clipping is the route to national, or even electoral, salvation.

When and if Congress, the administration and the public can be persuaded that national power to abuse the domestic money supply is not worth the candle, then our negotiators can zero in on the real issue: the world money supply. In 1967 President Johnson attempted to fight a war in Vietnam without raising taxes at home. The resulting increase in U.S. money supply was transmitted throughout the world, because in those days of fixed exchange rates every other country felt obliged to buy dollars and increase its reserve base in order to maintain its ordained exchange parity.

Even worse were the years 1971-72, when the Fed turned the money taps on full, flooding the world with unwanted greenbacks. Of course it can be argued that such a tidal wave of money was not the sole cause of world inflation: wage demands, Arab sheikhs and government fiscal profligacy have all played their roles. But, an increased money supply is the *sine qua non* for inflation. You cannot have higher prices across the board unless enough money is printed to pay them. And if you print more money than there are goods and services upon which it can be spent, prices will rise.

Finally, you cannot have an interdependent trading and financial world with independent, and irresponsible, national monetary policies. The lesson of the gold standard was that no nation could get away with unilaterally manipulating its money supply.

Thus, the reality behind the code words of negotiation on the international monetary system boils down to this: can the world money supply be stabilized? The answer is yes, *if* we Americans, who provide most of it, can bring ourselves to shed that useless, indeed pernicious, appendage of national sovereignty: coin clipping. If we can do so, we can lead the way to rational control of world money.

A Risk in Pontificating

Ever since the God of Moses chastised those early economists who deemed gold fit for sculpting into calves, it has been risky to pontificate upon the role of this mystic metal. The "gold bugs" advocate its restoration—at current market prices, of course—as the centerpiece of the international monetary system. Unfortunately, their motives may not always be Simon-pure. One suspects a wish to lock in profits by having the current market price guaranteed through central bank buying.

However, their call for a return to the "discipline of gold" reflects a very valid skepticism regarding political control of the money supply. The important point of this argument is not the exaltation of gold but rather the limitation of world money supply. Once that has been agreed upon, human ingenuity can doubtless devise ways by which gold could again be used to provide its traditional and important psychological backing for currency. Gold can be phased in once sanity has been restored, not vice versa.

Failure to restore monetary sanity will probably bring back gold—but only after the wreckage of today's currencies. Gold can be our servant or our master.

If and when control is regained over the money supplies behind the world's major currencies, the question of fixed versus floating exchange rates, like the role of gold, will fall into line. With unrestrained money growth, fixed exchange rates are an impossibility. But, once we have rigid, internationally-applied limitations on the money supply growth rates of each major currency, exchange rate parities will tend to stabilize and be easily maintained.

In practice, the way this could be worked is through creation, on American initiative, of a Class A membership in the International Monetary Fund open to all who would agree to allow their money supplies to grow within some formula rate, such as their collective real GNPs, with some leeway to allow for the state of the world business cycle. The Brazils and Britains could remain Class B members, allowing their currency parities to plummet as their money supplies soar, but when each nation came to its senses it could join the club.

Our Federal Reserve Board would lose its vaunted control, which it has so systematically and disastrously abused, over the domestic money supply, but it would gain a very influential voice in the formation of world monetary policy. More importantly, we have the opportunity to substitute reason for nightmare and nostrum. Perhaps thereby, we can ensure that our societies are saved from monetary, financial, social and political—in a nutshell, inflationary—collapse.

READING 10

Global Money Growth and Inflation

ARTHUR B. LAFFER

The inflation and recession of recent years are clearly a world phenomenon, affecting all the developed nations with only minor differences. Talk of economic "interdependence" is widespread. Yet economic policy is usually thought of on a national basis, as if the economies of different nations were only loosely connected.

This is particularly true of policies to control inflation. Experience ought to be teaching us that economists can no longer focus exclusively on domestic factors to explain domestic inflation. While such a narrow view may have been appropriate at some time in the past, it clearly no longer is. What is even more important about the world-wide view of inflation, as opposed to the closed-economy view, is that the policy implications are very different.

One can imagine that somehow the monetary authorities can control a closed economy's money supply—say demand deposits plus currency. In the world economy, control, as a practical matter, borders on inconceivable and, most assuredly, has not been practiced in recent years. The role of any one country's monetary authority—such as the U.S. Federal Reserve Board—wanes dramatically in the perspective of the world.

Money is, after all, one of the easiest commodities to move across national borders. Individual banks and other financial institutions operate in numerous U.S. and foreign locations. Even when the foreign operations are not direct subsidiaries, correspondent relationships and other close associations have been developed. The money markets not only within the United States but also in the world economy are closely interrelated by this vast financial network. Even the recent advent of floating exchange rates has not led to the dissolution of integrated money markets. With spot and forward foreign exchange markets, floating rates, at most, have only added somewhat to the costs of operating in those markets.

In the light of the ease with which money can be moved across borders and translated from one currency to another, it would seem that any anti-inflation policy will have to concentrate on the *world* money supply. No such figure is regularly available, and in trying to construct it there are numerous problems with the data. But in work at the University of Chicago, Jamie Chico and I have constructed a statistical series measuring the world money supply in terms of U.S. dollars.

Our series defines world money as the domestic money supplies of 15 major countries plus net Eurodollar deposits. Domestic money supplies (demand deposits plus currency) were converted into dollar amounts using appropriate exchange rates. Details of this definition of world money are discussed below.

We have also constructed similar series for world GNP and world inflation, also defined in dollars, covering the same 15 countries. World GNP was simply the sum of every country's GNP converted into dollars. World-wide inflation was merely the average of changes in foreign consumer price indices, after conversion to dollars and weighting the size of each country's GNP.

These three series are closely associated. See, for example, the following chart on world money growth measured in dollars. Of course, the close correspondence of data tells us nothing about whether money expansion causes world-wide income growth and inflation or whether the reverse is true. There can be little doubt, however, that these series do follow each other closely.

Indeed, the world-wide series are more

WORLD MONEY GROWTH AND WORLD INFLATION

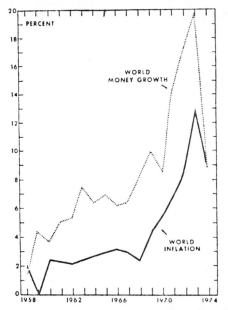

The growth of the world money supply—the domestic money supplies of 15 nations converted into dollars plus Eurodollar deposits—compared with the world inflation rate—also measured in dollars.

closely associated than comparable series for the United States alone. Therefore, based on data, as well as theory, the world-wide view of inflation appears more relevant to real events than its closed-economy counterpart.

Any strategy to control world money growth will have to be based on an understanding of the various sources of growth. I like to think of four: The U.S. money supply, the domestic money supplies of other nations, the Eurodollar market and the effect of exchange-rate changes.

The effects of domestic money supplies

are no doubt familiar to most readers. When the money supply of the U.S. or any other nation increases, this will also represent an increase in the world money supply, other things being equal. Others might prefer to use some measure of domestic money other than demand deposits and currency, particularly for purposes of strict comparison with Eurodollar deposits. This would somewhat increase the weight of domestic money supplies in the world money supply, but would change no basic conclusions.

Since Eurodollar deposits are not included in the domestic money supply of any nation, they have to be included separately in the world money supply. The inclusion of Eurodollars is particularly important because they have systematically moved in the opposite direction from the effect of domestic money supplies.

That is, if the effect of domestic money supplies is to increase the growth rate of the world money supply, then the Eurodollar effect is to decrease the total growth rate, and vice versa. In 13 of the last 15 years, for example, the growth rate of Eurodollars has risen when the growth rate of the U.S. money supply slowed, and slowed when the U.S. growth rate rose. It is as though Eurodollars were deliberately offsetting efforts of monetary authorities.

Ideally, we would have preferred to include not only Eurodollars but Eurocurrency deposits everywhere in the world. Unfortunately, the lack of readily available historical data precludes this. Given the lack of precision of the existing data, even this major exclusion should not alter the qualitative implications of our results. If anything, the inclusion of non-dollar Eurocurrencies plus dollar liabilities outside Western Europe should greatly strengthen the implications of the following analysis.

The final source of growth in the world money supply results solely from our choice of using the U.S. dollar as the unit of measurement for the world money supply. Even if Eurodollars and each country's supply remain unchanged, a devaluation of the dollar relative to other currencies will imply an increase in the dollar value of the world's money supply. Conversely, of course it will imply a decrease in the foreign currency value of the world's money supply.

To illustrate, let me imagine that there are 100 German marks and the exchange rate is four marks to the dollar. Thus, the dollar value of these 100 marks is 25 dollars. If the dollar devalues to the point where there are two marks to the dollar, then the dollar value of the 100 marks now equals 50 dollars. Thus even if the supply of marks is stable, they would contribute twice as much to the world money supply measured in dollars.

The exchange rate effect depends solely on the specific currency that is used to measure the world money supply. If measured in a generally appreciating currency, say the mark, world money growth would be slower. Correspondingly, world inflation *as measured in marks* would also be lower. The sole reason for using dollars is that we felt more people

were concerned with dollar inflation than inflation in any other single currency.

On the following chart all four of these
sources are plotted over the time interval.
Series one represents the effect on world
money supply growth of the U.S. money supply alone. Series two adds in the effect of
the other countries' domestic money supplies.
Series three adds in the additional effect of
Eurodollars. Finally, series four adds in the
final effect —that of exchange-rate changes—
to get the overall rate of growth of the
world money supply.

SOURCES OF WORLD MONEY GROWTH

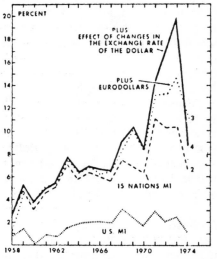

Series one is the U.S. domestic money supply (demand deposits plus currency). Series two adds the domestic money supplies of 14 other developed nations,
translated into dollar amounts at appropriate exchange
rates. Series three adds Eurodollar deposits. Series four
includes the effect of the movement in the exchange
rates of the dollar.

In recent years the most striking feature of these four sources is the insignifi-
cance of the U.S. money supply growth to

the growth rate of the world's total. In the past five years the U.S. money supply growth has never accounted for as much as 25% of the total money supply growth. In each and every year for the past five years, money supply growth rates of countries other than the U.S. were well over twice as important as U.S. money supply growth. Save one year, Eurodollars were more important than U.S. domestic dollars. In three out of the five years, the effect of exchange rate changes was more important then U.S. money supply changes.

Without making any excuses for particular policies of the Federal Reserve System, it would seem hard to justify single-minded attention to the U.S. money supply on the basis of this evidence. In the first place, the bulk of the evidence points to inflation as a world-wide phenomenon and not as an isolated U.S. occurrence. In the second place, it does not appear as though the U.S. money supply has, in practice, had much of an effect on the rate of monetary expansion in the world. Far more important for dollar inflation than Fed actions are foreign money supply growth rates, Eurodollar growth rates and changes in the dollar value of foreign currencies. The U.S. has little, if any, control over these sources of growth.

To extend even further the point that the U.S. has little control over the world money supply growth, we can compare the combined effect of all 15 domestic money supplies (including the U.S.), the effect of Eurodollars and the effect of exchange rate changes for the period 1958 through

1974. Up through 1968 domestic money supply growth rates dominated the growth rate of the world money supply and the effects of the other two factors were, at best, slight. Since 1968 Eurodollars have added more than 2% to the growth rate of the world money supply every year and cumulatively have increased the world money supply by almost 20% in the last six years. And as mentioned previously since Eurodollar growth rates have moved in the opposite direction from domestic money supplies, this source of money growth has tended to offset the actions of national monetary authorities.

Even on a world-wide basis, one is hard pressed to be sanguine about the ability of the world to control inflation. Without major institutional changes, much of the world's monetary expansion is outside of the control of monetary authorities. With the freeing of exchange rates and the rapid expansion of Eurodollars the monetary authorities' roles have diminished sharply.

Within the framework described here, inflation is a world-wide phenomenon. Individual countries' policies appear far less potent for combatting inflation than is currently believed. As far as I can tell, the best hope for controlling inflation is to reestablish control over the world's monetary growth. In order to do this it is obvious that domestic restraint has to be exercised. In addition to domestic monetary restraint, monetary authorities must also control the effects of exchange rate changes and Eurodollars. This means that movement toward more fixing of exchange rates and action to

control the expansion of Eurocurrency liabilities must be part of a viable strategy to
combat world inflation.

READING 11

Fear of Floating

HERBERT STEIN

The Secretary's chair was comfortable.
In fact, the whole room was comfortable.
The view from its windows was command-
ing. Through the west window he looked
down at the White House, with the typical
condescension of a successful banker for
an elected politician. And looking slightly
to the right he was assured by the cool por-
trait of Alexander Hamilton of his lineage
in the aristocracy of talent.

Still, the Secretary was uneasy. In a
few minutes the Under Secretary would
come in with the day's final report on the
exchange rate of the dollar. The Secretary
had come to dislike those reports in-
tensely. The idea of wondering each day
what the dollar was worth was distasteful
to him. And it was especially distasteful
when the dollar went down for days in a
row.

How things had changed since that deci-
sive meeting in this room in March 1973, in
the week when the world began to float. He
had been Deputy Secretary then, one of a
group of six or seven government officials
who had been meeting quietly over several
weeks to decide what to do next about the
dollar. Some were ideological floaters,

whose thinking began, and pretty much ended, with the idea that whatever the free market did was right. Others, more eclectic and claiming to represent real experience, were worried, although they could not articulate their concerns precisely.

On the last day the Secretary had turned to him. "Bill, you've spent most of your life in the financial markets. What do you think would happen? Would we get wild speculation? Would currencies be rising and falling all over the place, so that nobody could get any international business done?"

He had had a ready answer for that question then. "No, sir, Mr. Secretary. The markets will not be wild. The markets are rational, not emotional. You may get some swinging around from day to day, and maybe more than that at the beginning. But they'll settle down and reflect the fundamental forces, which is what you want."

And so they had floated, or, rather, had acquiesced in the rest of the world's floating. Everyone had not been convinced, but those who were reluctant saw that they would have to wait for another day.

A Big Surprise

The greatest surprise had been how large the fluctuations in the foreign exchange market were. Since he had become Secretary, all the markets, not just the foreign exchange market, looked emotional to him. Perhaps it was inevitable that what seemed a rational reaction to a real development if you were a private trader would seem an emotional response to a passing breeze if you were Secretary of the Treasury.

The dollar was still as high relative to most currencies as when the decision had been made to float. But there had been weeks and even months when it was down, down, down. Not just down against the D-mark, and the Swiss franc and the French franc. Even down against the pound and the lira. The ex-President had said, in a moment of distraction, that he didn't give an expletive-deleted about the Italian lira. He wished he could say the same.

Was the dollar down against the Cambodian what? What is the Cambodian currency—yuan, lei, franc, dollar? It had never occurred to him before. Could we do a financial Mayaguez? We could sell the Cambodian whatever-it-is short, and show that we're still a great financial power. Well, that was silly.

Everything had become so complicated. Two years ago they had talked about a clean float—a zipless float as someone later said. Governments would keep their hands off and let exchange rates find their own level in response to private demand and supply. But it hadn't worked out like that. Governments not only hadn't kept their hands off but it had become hard to tell what it meant to keep hands off.

In the middle of 1973 some people, who hadn't wanted to float in the first place, began to express concern that the dollar was falling lower than it had any good reason to. They thought we ought to show some confidence in the dollar, by buying some, so that others would have more confidence too. That had provoked some resistance within the Administration, from people who thought it was the opening gambit to get us back on the fixed-rate system. But we agreed to do a little, and in fact did a little, and it seemed to work. Later we did more, and other countries did also.

That was only the most obvious kind of dirtiness in the float. Governments do hundreds of things that affect the exchange rates, or might. Was it clean to affect the rates without meaning to, but dirty if you meant to do it? When the Chairman of the Fed said that he didn't want more rapid monetary expansion because that would depress the dollar, was that a dirty thought?

What good had it all done? The economists, including some who had prescribed floating as the quick fix, were beginning to have their doubts. They agreed that we hadn't had a monetary crisis since we started floating. But exchange rate uncertainty had increased the cost of international business. And floating had not brought everybody into balance. It hadn't stopped the world inflation. And it hadn't made everybody independent of everybody else.

Of course, that's the way economists are—never satisfied. But now even some of his downtown banker friends, who had gone for floating when it was fashionable, were grumbling. What they had really wanted was the end of the capital export controls, and now that they had that they would be just as happy to go back to the simpler life of the fixed exchange rate.

The sideways glances he got from his old New York friends didn't bother him nearly as much as the looks he got from his new friends in Paris, London, Bonn, Tokyo and other stops on the Finance Ministers' circuit. The U.S. Secretary of the Treasury used to be the top dog in the Group of Five, the Group of 10, the Group of 20, and all the other Groups. But now he sat below the salt, with all the other soft currency countries. Worse, he was the architect of softness.

It was too much, intolerable, insulting. Not for him personally. He didn't care. But for the country. The U.S. is a Great Power.

The buzzing intercom interrupted his thought. "Yes, send him in."

The Under Secretary crossed the room to the desk and handed him the typewritten sheet. It was like yesterday, and the day before. Down. Down against the mark, against the Swiss franc, and the French franc and the Belgian franc, and all the other francs.

He looked up at the younger man.

"What the hell is the Cambodian currency?"

"It's the riel."

"And how are we doing against the riel?"

"Down."

"Well, that's the end. We've got to stop this floating. Now you tell me what we have to do."

"But we went over that last week."

"I know. But tell it to me again. This time we're going to do it."

"First we would announce that we were

fixing the exchange rate of the dollar. Then if everybody believed us the private speculators would take care of the rest, buying when the dollar tended to fall, and vice versa.''

''But would they believe us?''

''I doubt it. After all, we have a record of devaluing and floating now that we didn't have years ago. And even then they didn't believe us. We'd have to be prepared to support the dollar.''

''And how would we do that? What would we do it with?''

''We could do it with gold. At present prices we have lots of gold. We could sell gold whenever we needed to get foreign currencies to use to buy dollars.''

''But there are an awful lot of dollars out there. And the price of gold won't stay where it is if we have to start selling.''

Irritating the Germans

''Maybe we could make an arrangement with other countries to buy gold from us at the present price when we need to support the dollar. But some countries— probably the Germans—wouldn't like that. They would be back in the position of having to take in gold or dollars and increasing their money supply when we ran a deficit. They would want us to bring our balance of payments into equilibrium, and in the long run that's the only solution anyway.''

''O.K. so we'll adjust. How do we do that?''

''One thing would be to squeeze down the economy, get the inflation rate down and slow down the growth of output.''

"You know I'm no inflationist. But we've already got about as tight a policy as the country will stand. There must be some better way."

"Yes, that's what all the Secretaries say. Back in the Sixties there used to be a lot of talk about the fiscal-monetary mix to deal with a recession and strengthen the dollar at the same time. We could run a bigger budget deficit and have tighter money. That would raise interest rates, keep dollars at home, and still support the economy with the deficit."

"What? Me go for a bigger deficit? You've got to be kidding."

"I thought you wouldn't like it. But we're near the end of the list. Would you like to think about controlling capital exports?"

"No."

"How about bringing the troops home from Europe. That's an old standby of these discussions."

"Henry wouldn't tolerate it."

The Secretary swung his chair around and looked out the window at the White House for a minute of silent thought. He turned his chair back half way and stared at ˙Alexander Hamilton for thirty seconds. Another half-turn and he faced the Under Secretary again. His mind was made up.

"We can't go on discussing this forever. We've got to decide. And I've come to a decision."

"What is it?"

"We'll go on floating."

"Right. See you tomorrow."

Chapter IV

The Re-emergence of Monetary Gold

From Money to Anti-Money

Gold has played a prominent part in monetary history. For a long time, gold *was* money; at other times the world's monetary system was based on the gold standard. Gold's role and its importance, however, have not been constant. Today, there is controversy whether gold will again be vital in monetary affairs or become just "another metal." In this chapter, gold will be the primary focus of attention. As an example of gold's chequered history, the metal which itself was once money or the basis for money is now viewed by some as the "enemy" of money, paper money that is.

The Gold Standard

Let us start with a definition. A gold standard exists when nations define their currencies in terms of gold and these currencies are fully convertible into gold. Under such an international monetary system relationships between currencies are defined by the value of each currency to gold. The adjusted process within this system is relatively simple, automatic, and apolitical. If a nation continues to import more than it exports and has a consistently large trade deficit, the national currency flows out until it returns as a demand on gold; this demand reduces the gold base for the domestic money supply and in turn leads to higher interest rates, a decrease in investment, less output, lower incomes, unemployment, recession, and possibly a depression. These repercussions in turn reduce demand for imports and thus balance trade. In the opposite situation, a nation with a continual and large trade surplus experiences a net gold inflow, expansion of the domestic money supply, lower interest rates, increased investment, employment and inflation. Inflation leads to a decrease in exports due to the higher prices and the trade surplus is eliminated. As can be seen, the domestic economy is the balance wheel of the adjustment process under the gold standard.

Critics of the gold standard point out that the national economy must endure harsh cycles of inflation and recession to reach equilibrium in the international trade and payment balances. In addition, the usefulness of the gold standard depends upon the quantity of gold in the world and the amount of gold produced each year. This can severely limit the growth of the world's money supply and thus limit trade and business growth as well. With South Africa as the major non-Communist source of gold, there are many sensitive political issues that emerge as well. The rather automatic operation of the gold standard makes it relatively apolitical and as such, an anathema to modern governments and politicians. In essence, paper money advocates believe that in a properly managed and functioning paper money system you can get the advantages of the gold standard (simplicity and stability) without the disadvantages.

Advocates of the gold standard point to its apolitical operation as one of its most positive features since it prevents nations from printing too much money and creating inflation. And gold standard advocates are quick to point out that even though the world has been off the gold standard since the 1930s, we have not been spared inflation, recessions, depressions and monetary crises.

During recent times of monetary crisis, some have advocated a return to the gold standard, which raises the questions, "Is the gold standard a realistic monetary alternative today?" and "How would it be implemented?" A return to the gold standard would require that overnight, all major nations agree to a fixed value for gold. This would have to be high enough to give them an adequate monetary base. Then all major nations would define their currencies in terms of gold and permit them to be freely convertible into gold. Each nation's money supply would be limited by its supply of gold. Care would have to be taken to get national economies in tune to avoid future economic calamities. The ever-present danger would be that governments would interfere with the gold standard by periodically raising the price of gold to permit monetary expansion. But this would prevent the system from operating effectively and would destroy confidence in it. Other suggestions have been made about how to implement a gold standard, one of the more interesting by Dr. Henry Hazlitt in a guest editorial in *Barron's* in October, 1975. He suggested that nations start on the path of economic reform first by balancing their budgets, and reducing their supply of new money, and that then the world would move naturally toward the gold standard.

Bugs and Spiders?

Gold still has an air of mystery. People continue to be fascinated by it, and to collect it for a number of reasons: as a hobby; as an investment; as a hedge against inflation; as the currency of the future; and as protection against catastrophic times ahead. Gold can be acquired in a number of forms: coins, jewelry, bullion and shares in gold mining companies. Gold advocates can be vocal and passionate and are often called "gold bugs"; those opposed are equally vocal and passionate (properly called "gold spiders"?). But the focus of this chapter will be upon the role of gold in international monetary affairs and not with other investment objectives associated with gold.

The American Gold Crawl

Two recent events increased the general interest in gold in the United States: the appearance of double-digit inflation and the end to the ban on private ownership of gold bullion. The ending of the ban was preceded by other events which indicated an increasing role for gold in monetary affairs. The following article analyzes recent gold history and the relationship of those events to the American legalization of gold bullion ownership.

READING 12

The Re-emergence of the Barbarous Relic: Gold *

Thomas G. Evans

January 1, 1975, ushered in a new year both chronologically and in terms of domestic and international monetary affairs. For, one day earlier, a historic event

* Published in *Wright Insights,* Vol. 4, No. 3, February 1, 1975 (Dayton Ohio: College of Business Administration, Wright State University). Reprinted with their permission.

took place in America—the ban on private gold bullion ownership ended. This ban, legislated by Congress during the Great Depression of the 1930s, has not dimmed the glitter of gold to Americans but limited their demand for gold to jewelry, coins, dental fillings, and the stock of domestic and foreign gold mining firms. But now, in the midst of a period of historically high inflation and recession, this ban has been lifted. The events subsequent to December 31, 1974, will tell much about the amount of pent-up American demand for gold bullion and the corresponding lack of confidence in paper money and our domestic economy. In addition, the role of gold in international monetary affairs and negotiations will also be greatly affected by the impact of American buying on the free market price of gold. Thus, "gold bugs" and businessmen alike will look with interest at the developments of 1975. It is the purpose of this article to review events leading up to 1975 to provide the perspective and background needed to analyze and understand recent and future gold developments and their implications.

Back in 1933, gold bullion and coin ownership by Americans was banned for two basic reasons: (1) to stop gold hoarding and inject dollars and demand into the depressed economy and (2) to prevent gains on the upcoming devaluation of the dollar from $21 to $35 per ounce. About a decade later, on the international scene, gold was to be further demonetized by the adoption of the dollar as a gold substitute. In the Bretton Woods Agreement in 1944 by which the International Monetary Fund was established and the world monetary system of fixed exchange rates was adopted, most major currencies were "pegged" to the dollar and that dollar pegged to gold. Dollars were freely convertible into gold at the rate of $35 per ounce. Given the problems of gold ownership (security, storage, and transportation) and the availability of dollars over time, the dollar began to replace gold as an international reserve asset.

The role of gold was quiet and stable until the late 1960s. In 1961, the "gold pool" was formed by the United States, United Kingdom, Belgium, Germany, Italy, the Netherlands, and Switzerland. These nations agreed to support the free market price on the London gold market at $35 per ounce by intervening with official reserves. During most of the 1960s, this worked smoothly and well. However, in early 1968, both increased demand and speculative pressures focused on gold and the "gold pool" nations sold massive amounts of gold from their official national reserves to keep the free market price down to $35. By March 1968, the outflows got so large that the pool decided to stop their support and a "two-tier gold market" developed in which the London free market price of gold was allowed to fluctuate according to supply and demand, but among the nations involved the official price was frozen at $35 and the nations agreed not to buy or sell gold to private parties. This was the first modern gold crisis.

The second crisis was related to the crisis of the American dollar in the early 1970s. The United States experienced a large gold outflow as "surplus dollars" from abroad were turned in for American gold. This process was halted by the historic events of August 1971 when the gold convertibility of the dollar was suspended, the dollar devalued, and the fixed-rate international exchange system modified by the Smithsonian Agreement reached in December 1971. The result of these events pushed up the price of gold on the London exchange in 1972 to the range of $60-$70.

The resulting monetary instability and turmoil renewed interest in the role of gold in monetary affairs over the next three years. The year 1972 was dominated internationally by efforts to keep the fixed rate exchange system established by the Smithsonian Agreement alive and well. Gold stayed in the background. Greater instability and turmoil re-emerged in 1973 as the Smithsonian Agreement collapsed and was replaced by a floating rate system while international monetary leaders searched for a more permanent solution to international monetary problems. During this search, a number of proposals involving a greater role for gold were made and a continuing barrier to progress was the issue of dollar inconvertibility into gold. In turn, these events were overwhelmed by the energy crisis of 1973-74 and the impact of increased oil prices on national economies and their international trade and payment balances. As instability increased and inflation grew, interest in gold correspondingly grew, a familiar pattern in monetary affairs today.

A critical development related to gold occurred in November 1973. The two-tier gold market, established in 1968, was terminated. The central banks of the gold pool nations agreed to end their ban on the sale of gold to private parties. This opened up a number of interesting possibilities but its immediate effect was to lower the free market price of gold since now nations could sell their gold in the free market at prices that had more than doubled since the ban had been established ($90 vs. the official price of $42). In retrospect, this was the first official event that represented a movement toward the remonetization of gold in monetary affairs. Each nation's gold reserves were "unfrozen" and available for use by that nation. Although uncertainty about future monetary developments and concern that the free market price of gold would rise even more in the future kept most of the official gold off the market, the glitter of gold in monetary affairs grew considerably brighter.

A second step was taken in June 1974, when the use of official gold reserves as collateral for international loans was allowed by the decision of the Group of 10 nations (the United States, Britain, France, West Germany, Italy, Japan, Canada, Belgium, the Netherlands, and Sweden) at their Washington meeting. A significant departure from previous attitudes was evident from the provision in the agreement that stated that the lender could value the gold reserves as collateral, which meant that the near market value would be used. This meant an official recognition of some other value for gold than its official value. In a practical sense, it gave some economically troubled nations a way of arranging additional national financing by further "thawing" out their gold reserves.

A third step also began in June 1974 when Congress began to press for an end to the American ban on gold bullion ownership. In August, President Ford signed into law the bill that ended by December 31, 1974, (barring any last-minute extension granted because of international monetary disruptions) the ban on private ownership of gold. Thus, American citizens were given notice of the opportunity for them to participate in what has become the "modern gold rush." Since August, the financial press has been full of ads for gold ownership and investment seminars and courses, gold manuals and books, offers and announcements of the opening of offices to handle gold purchases and sales, and advice and wisdom about buying and selling gold from various experts. Increased inflation and economic recession in the United States and abroad has further heightened this interest in gold and resulted in historically high prices for gold, near the $200 per ounce range. Gold is touted as the best hedge against inflation, a secure investment, and the best speculation for the future. Many experts predict that gold will hit $200 and beyond when Americans can own it. Others expect the price to peak at $200 and then decline as initial demand is met.

What are the implications and significance of these events and developments? Foremost, American citizens and firms can legally invest in gold bullion. But, as many experts pointed out as December 31 approached, this was easier said than done. Gold prices were climbing as December 31 drew near and one could expect to have to pay as much as a 10 percent premium over the market price for gold bullion for fees, insurance, transportation, etc. Additional expenses associated with bullion ownership include storage, security, and assaying. Thus, gold can become a very costly investment. In addition, to take advantage of lower fees, a large amount of gold must be purchased at one time and this would in turn require a large outlay since gold is expensive per ounce and the typical lots for gold investments are 10, 100, and 1,000 ounces. Margin requirements vary from 100 percent cash to above 10 percent for futures. Smaller lots are available (one, five, or less ounces) but these are not really suited for serious investment. Another consideration is that gold is a sterile investment, that is, no dividends can be expected. The only payoff is the expected increase in market price or potential use as money.

An additional danger in gold bullion investment is associated with the nature of the gold market. In a surprise move, the U.S. Treasury announced in early December 1974, that it was auctioning off 2 million ounces of U.S. gold reserves on January 6, 1975, in 400-ounce lots. This announcement quickly depressed the price of gold (down almost $9 within a day) and clearly shows the vulnerability of the "free market" price of gold to governmental intervention. Depending upon the market price on December 31, 1974, and thereafter, American firms and citizens may be purchasing gold bullion at near peak prices and therefore subject to quick reversals in future months, especially as governments may sell portions of their gold reserves to "stabilize" the gold market or reap a gain (that's why previous actions of nations to support gold and intervene in the gold market should be kept in mind today). Thus, with these risks and costs, one should not casually invest in gold bullion now that the American ban has been lifted. Equal cautions apply to plans to invest in gold coins and futures.

Prior to the Treasury announcement in early December, it appeared that the impact of the lifting of the American ban would be negative on the American economy and thus the lifting proved to be politically controversial. Since most of the gold that Americans could buy on December 31, 1974, would be imported, extensive investment would worsen the American balance of trade and payments and would also disrupt the domestic economy by draining funds from American financial institutions. Thus inflation and recession fighting would have been hindered by the flow of funds into gold. However, the Treasury announcement was hailed as an effort to prevent this, since Americans buying American gold from the government would keep the funds "at home." Concerns were still raised about the movement of funds from private financial institutions to the government but were countered with the claim that this would be offset by the resulting decrease in the government's need for funds from the investment market. The Treasury left open the door to future gold sales and thus we see how the termination of the two-tier gold market in 1973 and the lifting of the ban on American gold ownership in 1974 have been combined into a new tool for implementing American national economic policy.

The implications relating to the long-term role of gold in international monetary affairs are the least clear. If gold continues in 1975 to be a popular investment and if the price continues to climb, there can be little doubt that the trend toward the remonetization of gold will continue; but exactly how this will be manifested in future monetary agreements is not yet clear. At one extreme is the notion of a return to the gold standard but this is currently regarded as an extreme. However, what is clear is that the future role of gold in monetary affairs will be greatly conditioned by the short term impact of inflation, recession, uncertainty, and the ending of the ban on American gold ownership in 1975.

Historical Summary of Gold Developments

Date	Event	Primary impact on the role of gold
1933	Ban on American bullion ownership	Demonetization
1944	Bretton Woods Agreement	Demonetization
1961	Gold Pool Agreement	Demonetization
1968	Establishment of two-tier gold market	Remonetization
1971	Dollar convertibility ended	Remonetization
1973	Termination of the two-tier gold market	Remonetization
1974	Use of gold reserves as collateral	Remonetization
1974-5	Lifting of American ban on gold ownership	Remonetization

The degree of American interest (or lack thereof) in gold bullion was clearly eivdenced when gold went on sale in January, 1975. Nothing like a gold rush developed and to many the sale was a prime candidate for the "nonevent of the year" award. In all fairness, however, certain factors must be considered. To begin with, the adverse publicity given to the ownership of gold may have kept many away. Just prior to the sale, many financial leaders expressed caution and warned against the purchase of gold, even while promoters were touting its advantages. The overall impact was confusing. Second, the price of gold, as the ban ended, was at an historic high in anticipation of American demand. On December 31, 1974 gold stood at $197.50 per ounce.

In this kind of situation, large sales of gold to Americans should not have been expected. In fact, had Americans purchased large amounts of gold at the high price, it would have demonstrated a lack of investment knowledge. The atmosphere that surrounded the opening of the "gold box" to Americans was aptly captured in an editorial cartoon which appeared in a Dayton, Ohio paper on January 5, 1975.

The major U.S. governmental concerns associated with the lifting of the ban were that Americans would add to the payments deficit by purchasing foreign gold or that Americans would unwisely invest in a glamorous but economically unsound article. These quickly faded when Americans expressed little interest in gold once it became legal. Yet, at least as a precaution, the U.S. Treasury announced in early December, 1974, that on January 6, 1975, it would auction two million ounces of American gold (which represented less than 1% of the total American reserve) in 400 ounce bars. Bidding would be open to both American and foreign buyers with bids to be submitted 10 days prior to the auction. The U.S. Treasury made the comment that it would repeat the auction "from time to time." The obvious impact was a drop in the price of gold on the market. The Treasury's avowed motives were patriotic: if it didn't sell the gold, American dollars would flow

abroad and hurt our payments balance; additionally, it
was a new way to raise money to finance the government.
The reaction of the editors of the *Journal* to this
Treasury action appears on the following page in
Reading 13.

'Forget it . . . It's too speculative . . .'

*By Mike Peters for the Dayton Daily News, January 5, 1975
and used with permission.*

READING 13

The 'Barbarous Metal' Returns

We can endorse the Treasury's determination to free Americans to own gold and to bring this about in a reasonably orderly way through an auction of some of its own supplies to help accommodate initial demand.

This marks a healthier and more mature attitude towards gold and a movement away from the recent superstition that it is a barbarous metal best left buried in the ground. We do not doubt that gold has power to stir irrational dreams, but that is no reason to exorcise it through burial. As Bretton Woods demonstrated for nearly 20 years, it also can be a useful form of money if properly managed and understood.

That is not to say, however, that we have no troubling questions about the 2-million ounce gold auction the Treasury has scheduled for January 6. They can be summed up largely by asking where the Treasury plans to go from there.

We wonder, in particular, whether the Treasury has any explicit notion about the future role of gold in international monetary affairs. One can of course design international systems without gold, and in fact one can design a gold-based system without huge government hoards of the metal. But when the Treasury starts to sell gold it ought to know where it is going; if it slips into the habit of selling gold merely to cover federal deficits, it will simply invite Congress to spend up yet another national resource.

If the Treasury is absolutely sure the world ought to retain the current system of floating exchange rates, then of course the gold has no monetary role and should be sold in some orderly way. But while we have been sympathetic toward the experiment with floating rates, we have to admit that the world's economic experience since their advent has been far from a happy one. We certainly would not want to preclude a return to some form of fixed-rate system. And if you start to think of fixed-rate systems, you also do not want to preclude some possible role for gold.

Now, we doubt that the January 6 gold sale in itself would disturb any possibilities for reforming the world system. It affects less than 1% of the U.S. gold hoard. The sale is probably necessary, as the Treasury has argued, to prevent a sudden and possibly inflationary flight of American dollars to gold markets overseas after the U.S. ownership ban comes off December 31.

But after taking this initial step the Treasury should chart its course carefully before making further sales. Are we moving towards some orderly monetary plan or are we merely selling gold as a convenient way for the Treasury to deal with immediate problems?

The pattern in the U.S. for a decade has been for government to enhance its power through public policies that deplete human and physical resources. Much of the nation's store of natural gas has been used up, for example, on uneconomic purposes through artificial controls on price; over-consumption of other resources has been encouraged through a period of general price controls; government has grabbed a major chunk of the nation's capital and funnelled it into income transfer programs, at the same time crippling the nation's ability to form new capital. Inflation has been a concomitant to all this.

All other things being equal, the Treasury sale of gold to the public is not of itself inflationary and could even have a stabilizing effect. But we are concerned that all things would not long remain equal. A Congress that has not been characterized by self-restraint would soon see that here is yet another tool for the Treasury to use to disguise federal budget deficits. If that is to be the only goal of gold sales, it is one that could eventually leave the nation with little in the way of reserves and resources and much in the way of excess commitments.

As we said there is no reason to be afraid of gold, whatever its barbarous past. But there is reason to take warning from that past and overcome the notion that selling gold is the route to some new El Dorado.

The Gold Sale and
Auction Disappointments

The great American gold sale was a flop. Some of the nation's largest banks were amazed at the lack of demand. Even the Treasury auction six days later was a disappointment: instead of selling all two million ounces, only about 750,000 ounces were bid for, at an average price of approximately $166 per ounce. According to reports, the primary purchaser of this gold was a West German bank. Nevertheless, there are long term implications. The lifting of the American ban is bullish on gold insofar as Americans can participate in future gold rushes (such as developed in 1974 when inflation hit hard) and can push up the price of gold in competitive international markets. Treasury auctions tend to be bearish insofar as they increase the supply of gold available to Americans and foreigners alike and help keep the price of gold down or lower it. Of course, if the American demand for gold and the supply offered by the Treasury were equal, the events would cancel each other. But that is not likely.

The Gold War:

Auctions vs. Revaluations

Opposing the U.S. on the matter of gold, as well as in the fixed vs. floating exchange rate debate, France has been consistently in the forefront. In December, 1974, the French and American presidents met at Martinique and agreed that France could revalue its gold reserves at the current market price, rather than at the official price of $42.22 per ounce. Under the Bretton Woods Agreement, gold was originally the most imortant factor in international monetary affairs. As time passed, however, the dollar gained in prominence, and gold became less important. During the period covered by Bretton Woods, gold was officially valued at $35 per ounce. With the passing of Bretton Woods and the Smithsonian agreements and the two devaluations of the American dollar, the official value of gold inched up to $42.22. Meanwhile, the market price of gold at this time was almost five times greater, at approximately $190. Under the circumstances France wanted to value its official gold holdings at market prices instead of at the official rate. The only previously sanctioned departure of this type was the agreement among the Group of 10 nations in June, 1974, to allow a nation to value its gold reserves at market prices for purposes of collateral for international loans. This was a concession to Italy which needed financial aid and wanted to use its gold stockpile as collateral. France revalued its gold stock in January, 1975, using the market price of $170.40 and pledged to revalue its stock every six months based on the average price of gold for the preceding three months. In this way, France could continually emphasize the difference between the current market and official prices of gold.

France's actions represented a counter to the U.S. Treasury's auction of gold "from time to time," with each nation trying to advance its beliefs about the importance or lack of importance of gold in international monetary affairs. The official American position in recent monetary history has been "anti-gold." Yet to many, the American action in 1971 suspending the gold convertibility of the dollar was contrary to that position. If the Americans felt that gold was just another metal why didn't they continue giving up gold for dollars? The Treasury auction became a way to show that the Americans meant business and were willing to sell off American gold. But France was pro-gold and sought to get favorable publicity for gold and show that it meant business too. Thus, the two nations entered into a "gold war" using auctions and revaluations as the main weapons. In Round One, with the lack of much American interest in the Treasury auction, France won.

Was Gold Dying?

But France's victory was short-lived. After the failure of the U.S. gold sale and Treasury auction, the gold market became quiet. Then, after the first quarter of 1975, gold began a steady but gradual decline in price which surprised some people and satisfied others. In many respects, gold became part of a campaign against inflation, paper money and governments which printed money too easily and thus caused inflation. Throughout 1974, as inflation heated up, the price of gold became almost a panic index for those who were losing or had lost confidence in paper money. "Prophets of economic doom" played up this role for gold, and the prospect of U.S. gold sales aggravated the situation as gold's price rose too rapidly. It was only natural that a cooling off period would follow, as it did beginning in the second quarter of 1975. But to many the gradual decline in the price of gold meant that, monetarily, gold was dying or dead. The obituary notices, like those Samuel Clemens read about himself in the newspaper, were premature. As time wore on, the general interest in gold and its price dwindled —perhaps because gold had become oversold and overexposed, but not because it was terminally ill.

The Gold War: Round Two

By the middle of 1975, the price of gold had declined to $167 and the U.S. Treasury announced its second auction of gold, to be held at the end of June. This second auction was only for 500,000 ounces of gold and was a "Dutch auction" in which all of the successful bidders would pay the lowest acceptable price. Somehow, the auction coincided with the day on which France was scheduled to revalue its gold reserves. Reading 14 presents the opinions of the editor of *Barron's* on the subjects of the Treasury auction and the U.S.-France gold war.

READING 14

Gold War Gets Hotter

The U.S. Neither Deserves Nor Is Likely to Win

ROBERT M. BLEIBERG

Fatuous statements on the international monetary system and gold have been a dime a dozen in recent years, but every now and again a genuine collector's item surfaces. Thus, according to *The Milwaukee Sentinel* of November 24, 1967 (furnished us by William L. Law of the Cudahy Tanning Co., Inc., a genuine collector), Congressman Henry S. Reuss (D., Wis.), now chairman of the House Banking and Currency Committee, went on record at the time as saying: "with gold no longer playing a major role in the international monetary system, its price will sink to its value in the arts—something much closer to $6 an ounce rather than the current $35. . . ." Former President Nixon once called the short-lived, ill-fated Smithsonian "the greatest monetary agreement in the history of the world," while George P. Shultz, greatest Secretary of the Treasury since John Connally, told reporters at the annual meeting of the International Monetary Fund in Nairobi in the fall of 1973 that by July 31, 1974, the IMF would assuredly reach accord on a system to replace floating exchange rates: "You can pin us down on that."

George Shultz is long gone from the U.S Treasury, and global monetary reform remains as elusive as ever. Indeed, perhaps more so, for those whom he left behind, notably Jack

F. Bennett, Under Secretary for Monetary Affairs, seem equally given to making foolish statements in public and to taking positions which grow less defensible year by year. Ten days ago Mr. Bennett was in rare form. In announcing the proposed auction on June 30 of 500,000 ounces of U.S. gold, second such sale since the turn of the year, the Treasury official took pains to put the transaction in a favorable light. "We are selling something that belongs to the American people," he said earnestly, "and we want to get the best price for it." According to the newspapers, moreover, the Under Secretary denied that the timing of the abrupt announcement had anything to do with the increasingly acrimonious debate between the U.S. and some European countries over a new monetary system for the Western world and the future role of gold. "The proposed sale," Bennett averred, is "consistent with our position that gold has no monetary use in the future, but is otherwise unrelated to that argument."

Jack Bennett prudently stopped short of saying—as his predecessors were wont to do— that either the Special Drawing Right or the dollar is as good as gold. On all other counts, however, his remarks strike us as fatuous enough to rate a cherished place in Bill Law's collection. In the laudable effort to "get the best possible price," the Treasury (unlike last January, when it sold some bullion at bargain basement levels) this time plans to hold what is known in the trade as a "Dutch auction," whereby all successful bidders pay the same price. Yet mere announcement of the sale immediately served to depress the market by more than $5 an ounce, an impact reinforced by premature official word that if circumstances warrant, further sales will be made this year. As for the allegedly fortuitous timing, the auction will take place on the same day as France—perhaps the bitterest foe of Treasury policy—is scheduled to revalue her own gold reserves. "It's a shot across the bows," so Eliot Janeway (no gold bug, he) wrote in the latest issue of the Janeway Service. "I personally suspect," echoed James Dines, "that this . . . was a deliberate slap in the face to the French."

So the gold war between the U.S. and Western Europe (not just France, which says out loud what its Common Market partners are thinking) has grown hotter. It's a war which this country neither deserves nor is likely to win. To be sure, the U.S. Treasury persists in seeking to downgrade gold as just another commodity—porkbellies are the favorite analogy—or "something that belongs to the American people." Yet as syndicated columnist Alice Widener angrily pointed out the other day, "something" is defined by Webster's as "some undetermined or unspecified thing; not remembered or immaterial." That's scarcely the view of either West Germany which last year was willing to lend $2 billion on the strength of gold as collateral, or by hard-pressed Italy, which in consequence was enabled to buy the time needed to put its house in order. At $42.22 an ounce, gold constitutes a sizable percentage of international reserves. At a market-related quotation (which central banks at any time now may embrace), it's over half. Just how assets of such magnitude are to be "phased out" remains a mystery on which Washington refuses to shed light.

By doctrinaire hatred of the precious metal, finally, the Treasury willy-nilly has perpetuated the existence of floating exchange rates, a kind of semi-controlled chaos which, while not yet wholly justifying the worst fears of its detractors, has measured up neither to the hopes of its supporters nor the exigencies of the times. Far from leading to smooth, nearly imperceptible adjustments, floating exchange rates have created unprecedented turbulence in foreign exchange markets, stimulated further inflation and coincided with the worst slump in business activity since the Great Depression. *The Wall Street Journal* recently criticized "The Vacancy at Treasury," by which it meant the glaring failure of Secretary William Simon to take charge of international monetary policy. War may or may not be too important to be left to the generals, but it surely can't be left to lesser ranks.

Whether or not there are too many Indians at Treasury and too few chiefs, one pow-wow after another has yielded precious little progress. Nearly 12 months have passed since July 1, 1974—"You can pin us down on that" —and the Western world seems as deeply divided as ever. More precisely, by clinging to its anti-gold prejudice, the U.S. finds itself increasingly opposed to and isolated from the European Economic Community. It differs with the EEC over giving up veto power (20% or more of the total vote) in the International Monetary Fund. With scant support in any quarter, it wants the IMF to sell the bullion supplied by members and distribute the proceeds to the underdeveloped Third World. And it wants central banks to be free to sell gold thereby moving it into private hands, but not to buy.

Not surprisingly, France and the others—as they doubtless will reemphasize at the meeting of the IMF"s Interim Committee on Monetary Reform in Paris this week—will have none of such quixotic schemes. On the contrary (auction sale or no), they will doubtless press the U.S. for a further retreat from its extreme position on gold. On this score, the Europeans already have gained considerable ground. In 1974, as noted, Italy won a reprieve from financial disaster (one which she has put to surprisingly good use) by pledging part of its gold stock (at $120 an ounce) against a loan from West Germany. Last December, at a summit meeting in Martinique, France extracted U.S. agreement to its (and any other central bank's) revaluation of its gold holdings at a market-related price. The French promptly revalued at $170.40 an ounce, a figure which they will reappraise at month's end. Meanwhile, the EEC is pushing a plan whereby central banks—if all together they did not add to their holdings—would be free to buy gold as well as to sell.

None of this smacks of "phasing out" the precious metal—quite the contrary. And whatever the "printophiliacs in the U.S. Treasury" (as Jim Dines aptly has labeled them) may pretend, there is no substitute for gold. Surely floating exchange rates, with which the Western world has been trying to live and work since the collapse of Bretton Woods, aren't the answer. For one thing, the float has been exceedingly "dirty": by its own admission, the Federal Reserve "intervened in the foreign exchange market repeatedly in February 1975 and less often in March and April, selling $793.2 million equivalent of West German marks, Swiss francs, Belgian francs and Dutch guilders in the three months." Far from ironing out currency fluctuations, the float has aggravated them: around the turn of the year, the U.S. dollar in six weeks' time lost nearly 10% of its value against the stronger Western European moneys. And while a global depression—this time around, anyway—seems to have been averted, the float has led to a rash of bank failures and coincided with the worst inflation and subsequent recession of the postwar years. "If we don't reach agreement in Paris. . .," so Jack Bennett has been quoted as saying, "the world doesn't come to an end." Perhaps not, but it thereby persists—for no good reason—in living dangerously.

Reappraisal of U.S. intransigence, in sum, is long overdue. (On this score, even the Secretary of the Treasury, who reportedly will convene a group of monetary experts later this month to weigh the matter, may be having second thoughts.) And it's equally clear in what direction U.S. policy should go. As Milton Gilbert, longtime Economic Adviser to the Bank for International Settlements, last year told a conference at Arden House sponsored by the Committee for Monetary Research & Education: "I believe strongly that the primary overall need of the system is to have a restoration of the convertibility of the dollar. This would constitute the first step to rebuilding public

confidence in the dollar and would give some
hope that we might again reach a system of
'stable but adjustable parities.' If instead,
we continue on the line that gold should be
phased out, we will find that stable exchange rates will be phased out also."

Surprisingly to many, including the Treasury
officials, this second auction was quite successful and over 750 bids were received. All gold offered
was sold for a price of $164 although again, most of the
gold was purchased by foreign interests. The U.S. received $82 million from the sale. Also interestingly,
this auction had little impact on the gold market on
June 30, presumably since it was well-anticipated. In
view of the decline in the price of gold since January, however (and France's revaluation of its gold
reserves emphasized this,) Round Two went to the
U.S.

Gold's Price and Fixing

Reference to Appendix A, Foreign Exchange and
Price of Gold, shows how gold did during 1975 and
clearly, after rising steadily in the first quarter,
the price of gold declined until October, 1976 when
it began to rise again. In the whole period for gold
in the appendix, notice that gold's price hit its
peak in December, 1974 after the historically high inflation of 1974 and just prior to the American legalization of bullion ownership. Comparing the price of
gold at the end of 1974 with the beginning of 1974,
gold almost doubled in 12 months.

The way the price of gold is established is interesting and relevant since the "market price" is
not established in quite the same way as the market

price of currencies or securities. Instead, in London, the major gold market, five major bullion dealers meet twice a day to consider all the supply and demand factors for gold and "fix" a price which is quoted around the world. These dealers are experts and take a macro view toward gold in setting the price which reflects their expert opinion of a price which equates supply with demand.

The IMF Gold Sale Proposal

The year 1975 also became a year of "garage sales" of gold. As previously covered in Chapter II, the IMF Interim Committee of 20 met in January, 1976 in Jamaica and a major outcome of this meeting was a proposal that the IMF sell part of its gold stockpile to provide financial aid to needy nations. This gold stockpile of the IMF came from the "initiation fee" nations paid when they joined the IMF, 25% in gold and 75% in their own national currency.

The preliminary work on this proposal was done by the IMF's Monetary Negotiations Committee which met in September, 1975 just prior to the annual meeting of the IMF in Washington. Its proposal on gold was contingent on the ability of the Interim Committee to reach agreement on currency matters at its January, 1976 meeting. The Monetary Committee proposed the sale of 25 million ounces of gold back to member nations who originally contributed them, and the abolition of the official price ($42.22) of gold. The Group of 10 industrial nations also met in Washington concurrently and in a related move agreed that central banks could increase their gold reserves as the IMF decreased its reserves through the proposed sale.

These gold proposals were the major outcome of the 1975 annual IMF meeting and were acceptable to all factions. The U.S. was pleased, believing that the IMF sale would further demonetize gold and was consistent with the U.S. Treasury sales. France was pleased that now it could buy more gold from the IMF for its reserves and regarded the proposed abolition of the official price of gold as consistent with France's "pioneering" practice of using the current value to value its gold stock. The needy nations were happy that finally there was agreement on a means of providing them with desperately needed financial assistance in a way that had no political strings attached.

The only ones who weren't happy about the IMF move were the gold bugs. The announcement of the proposed IMF sale of 25 million ounces did what the second U.S. Treasury auction did not do: it knocked about $5 from the price of gold that day. In fact, by the end of the following week, gold had sunk to a 12-month low.

The Price of Gold—
Recent Causal Factors

Sufficient recent gold history has now been covered to permit a consideration of those factors which have emerged as modern influences on the price of gold.

(1) As a historically accepted store of value and money, during times of economic instability, uncertainty, or turmoil the demand for gold and its price tend to increase. Conversely, during times of economic stability, prosperity, and peace the price of gold tends to drop.

(2) During times of inflation, confidence in paper money fades and the demand for gold increases and boosts the price. Surprisingly, during a recession, gold does not behave in a similar way; in fact, recessions tend to lessen the demand for gold, especially from the speculative standpoint.

(3) The supply of gold, in the main, comes from

the nation of South Africa. The central government is concerned with the market price since this determines how much South Africa will get from its major export. In recent years, South African production of gold has been approximately 700-800 million ounces per year.

(4) The industrial demand for gold, although small, is stable, has grown steadily from year to year, and has great potential.

(5) An unknown but powerful influence is the Soviet Union, which produces gold and uses it to purchase "hard currencies" to finance imports. Obviously, the amount of Russian gold output per year, its national reserves of gold and its selling plans are secret. But the Russian potential to influence the price of gold is considered great.

(6) Another potentially powerful influence is the amount of gold held by Middle Eastern OPEC nations in their national reserves.

A Dirty Float for Gold?

Given the lessening of inflation in 1975, the outbreak of the world-wide recession, and the announcement of the impending IMF gold sale, the price of gold was doomed to drop. But the plans of the IMF coupled with the U.S. Treasury announcement that it would sell gold "from time to time" raised some long-term concerns. One possibility was the end of the free market for gold and a return to a controlled gold market with some new twists. What could develop, in this view, might be similar to the dirty or managed float of the currency markets, where national governments intervene to keep the price of their national currencies within internally known bounds. The IMF and Treasury plans could create a parallel situation in the gold market since the mechanisms for a dirty float already existed. When this became apparent, the price of gold dropped approximately $12 within 10 days and continued to decline.

Additional facts about the proposed sale of IMF gold became clearer in late December, 1975. The Group of 10 industrial nations (the United States, Canada, Belgium, France, West Germany, Italy, Japan, Britain, the Netherlands, and Sweden) met and agreed that the Bank for International Settlements could be used to purchase IMF gold for central banks which wanted it. The BIS was established in 1930 with seven member nations as a part of the Young Plan to assist in the settlement of financial claims arising out of World War I. After serving as the clearing house for war reparations, it continued as an important agency for the collaboration of Western central bank governors and for the study of international financial problems. The BIS is an observer to the IMF and has worked together with both the IMF and the Group of 10 on monetary issues. Now the BIS could act as the gold buying agent for any of the Group of 10 nations and thus prevent outsiders from knowing which nations were buying gold or how much.

In January, 1976, the IMF Interim Committee of 20 met in Jamaica, agreed on the gold sale proposal and recommended it to the 128 member nations of the IMF (the meeting is described in Chapter II). However, it was expected to take some time before the proposal could be implemented and the immediate impact of this decision on the price of gold was minimal.

The whole package was presented to the IMF Board of Governors on April 30. In May the IMF announced plans to begin the gold auction in early June by selling 780,000 ounces of gold at market-related prices and to follow with similar auctions every six weeks over a four-year period until all of its 25 million ounces were sold. The gold was to be sold in lots of 2,000 ounces and the names of the successful bidders would not be disclosed. It was indicated that central banks would not be allowed to bid for this gold but that the BIS would. The IMF made it clear that it was not concerned with what happened to the gold once it was sold.

The First Four Auctions

Once the IMF auctions began, the price of gold was greatly affected. The first auction on June 2, unlike the first U.S. Treasury auction, sold all 780,000 ounces of gold at a common price of $126 per ounce. A second auction of equal size followed on July 14 and again, all the gold was sold, this time at $122 per ounce. The decline in the price of gold is evident from the change in the successful bid price over the six-week period. On the "free market" just before the second IMF auction, gold hit a 30-month low of $121.85. Just the week before, France again revalued its national gold supply. In the face of sinking prices, she ended up in the embarrassing position of writing down her national gold stock by $605 million, clearly a sound defeat in the U.S.-French gold war now that the IMF had entered on the side of the United States. By August, 1976, there were predictions that gold would continue to slide until it reached a floor somewhere under $100. Correspondingly, currencies were generally strong as gold declined.

Some changes were announced in August for the September IMF gold auction. In the first and second auction, the gold was sold to all successful bidders at the same price and the names of all successful bidders were held in confidence. For auction number three, the IMF said it would sell gold at various prices above a "secret floor" to all successful bidders and that it would disclose the identity of the successful bidders but not the quantity of gold they purchased.

By September, 1976, however France had enlisted some "allies" in its gold war with the United States and the IMF. Five days before the third auction, the Common Market nations contacted the IMF and asked for a slowdown in the sales. This was widely interpreted as a call by the Common Market nations for the IMF to "cool it" on its sales of gold because the market price of gold was decreasing. Both Italy and West Germany were concerned because Italy had pledged its gold reserves as collateral for West German loans. Thus, three Common Market nations had a stake in the price of gold. The request was interpreted as a long term one and the upcoming third auction was not in question. But the Common Market did let the IMF know that it was concerned with the impact of the future sales of gold on the price of gold. And it also indicated that France was enlisting allies in its fight over gold with the U.S., just as the U.S. had apparently enlisted the IMF on its side. As might be expected, South Africa also expressed concern about the recent trend in gold's price. The issue shaped up as a controversial topic at the annual IMF meeting in October, 1976 in Manila.

The third IMF auction went off as planned and was a success in many respects. The day before the sale, the price of gold dropped $3, reflecting the uncertainty of major gold dealers about what "floor price" the IMF would adopt. All 780,000 ounces of IMF gold were sold, at an average price of $109.40. Most of the sales went to major private bullion dealers, major Swiss and West German banks, and others. Surprisingly, the BIS was not on the list of successful bidders. The market price of gold was not significantly different from the sale price of $109.40 and the floor price of $108.76.

In fact, this third auction had a bullish effect on the price of gold because: (1) the gold was sold easily, indicating strong demand; (2) it was sold mainly to private bidders, indicating broad demand; and (3) the sale price and floor price were not significantly different from the current market price. In addition, during the recent price decline, some individuals sold gold short and needed to purchase gold to complete their contracts. All these factors, including some general relief that the third auction was over, pushed up the price of gold approximately $8 within five days of the auction. But the request of France and the other Common Market countries was apparently ignored in that the IMF planned the fourth auction for October 27, as originally scheduled.

This third auction was critically important, given the changes in format and the adoption of a "floor price" by the IMF. The decline in the price of gold before and the rise after the auction differed from the pattern of the two previous auctions. But there was still uncertainty about the real purpose of the IMF auctions: if they continued to push down the price of gold then the amounts realized from the sales and available to poor nations would decrease, counter to an avowed purpose of the auctions. Time would tell whether the IMF gold auctions were designed to help poor nations or just a control mechanism put on the market price of gold.

The fourth auction was held as scheduled in October and was as successful as the third. There was broad demand for the gold and this also had a bullish effect on the market price of gold thereafter.

Gold's Future

Certainly, the general decline in the price of gold in 1975-76 has raised some new questions about the role of gold in monetary affairs. As a result of the recent decline, the gold bugs have been silenced, at least until the next round of double-digit inflation and economic tribulation. In addition, France has been embarrassed by its pro-gold position. Meanwhile, opinions differ as to whether the current price of gold is realistic or artificially low. Personal opinions aside, it is clear that gold still commands monetary respect and has not lost its traditional appeal.

As evidence of the critical but unseen role of gold, consider a study done by Richard C. Young of Hoening & Strock, an international services firm. He found that from the end of 1970 to the end of 1974, four currencies that could be considered the strongest also had a higher proportion of gold backing than the weaker currencies: Switzerland, the Netherlands, Austria, and West Germany. This was reported in the "Heard on the Street" column in the April 7, 1975 *Journal* Mr. Young disavowed any pro-gold motivation in the study but the results speak for themselves.

If gold is not to be a keystone in future monetary arrangements, then what is? Something is needed that provides stability and serves as a benchmark in a monetary system. A logical candidate is the SDR, created primarily as a substitute for gold and dollars and often called "paper gold." The Special Drawing Right was created by the IMF in 1969 as a reserve and liquidity asset. A little more than nine billion dollars' worth of SDRs were allocated to IMF member nations during the period of 1970 to 1972. SDRs are not currency but represent bookkeeping entries within the IMF"s books. They were to be used primarily in the settlement of balance of payment deficits among member nations. The IMF nations agreed to accept SDRs in exchange for convertible currencies. Initially, the SDR was valued at a little less than a gram of gold which then was equal to one dollar.

A major change in the value of the SDR took place on July 1, 1974 when its basis was shifted from the dollar to the average value of a composite ("basket") of 16 weighted currencies. These included the U.S. dollar, British pound, French franc, West German mark, Japanese yen and others. By releasing the SDR from the direct fluctuation of the dollar alone, the SDR's value gained greater stability.

Although the SDR was created primarily for transactions between IMF nations at a high monetary level, it became increasingly popular in commercial transactions in the latter half of 1974 and in 1975 after its revaluation; for example:

(1) In June, 1975, Ministers of the Organization of Petroleum Exporting Countries (OPEC) decided to change the pricing of oil from U.S. dollars to SDRs.

(2) In June of 1975, the first issue of SDR denominated Eurobonds was sold.

(3) The major airlines of the world proposed that future passenger fares, cargo rates, etc. be quoted in SDRs.

(4) A major New York bank in August, 1975, announced plans to make loans and accept deposits denominated in SDRs.

But beyond these applications, no widespread popularity has developed for the SDR and little has been proposed about its role in future monetary arrangements. There have been a few suggestions during previous currency crises that an SDR-based world monetary system be developed, but little progress has been made in that direction. Thus, the SDR does not appear to be more popular than the gold which it was to replace. However, the IMF has the option to create more SDRs at any time, provided it gets the concurrence of 85% of the weighted vote in the IMF.

Chapter V

A New Era

The Current Situation

Today, we are in a new era of international monetary affairs. Changes in the basic structure of the world's monetary system within the past five years have produced a new system with the following major characteristics:

(1) Currency values are floating, with governmental interventions.

(2) There are no standard references—not a given currency, gold, nor the SDR.

(3) There is no operating international monetary agreement, such as the Bretton Woods or Smithsonian agreements.

(4) The role of gold is uncertain but active.

(5) Recent monetary negotiations have failed to bring about solutions to monetary crises or world economic problems.

(6) Major economic power is now in the hands of many groups, some not traditionally economic leaders in the world (i.e. OPEC and Third World nations).

Of great importance is the process by which this new system developed. It was not by the orderly, planned evolution of monetary progress through negotiation. Instead, it was created by a series of unplanned and unexpected monetary crises. After five years we are just beginning to see stability return to the currency markets. And even with this stability, no one can be sure that the causes of the recent monetary crises have been successfully dealt with and will not re-emerge to cause turmoil again.

Today, we still have many vital issues in monetary affairs which are controversial and unresolved: the dollar overhang; fixed vs. floating exchange rates; the relationship between currency changes and changes in national trade and payment balances; the role of gold; and the future of the SDR. Can lasting monetary progress be achieved until these issues are settled? It is very doubtful.

The recent experience with the Smithsonian Agreement has taught us an important lesson in contemporary monetary affairs. In retrospect, this agreement was a quickly arrived at solution to a major problem. Unfortunately, the solution only slightly modified the existing monetary system and did not go far enough in treating the major problems. It collapsed quickly, and created even greater turmoil. Perhaps if currencies had been allowed to float longer and more time taken to examine the problems with the Bretton Woods system, a more permanent solution might have been found.

Given this lesson and the sensitivity of currency markets today, future monetary progress is apt to be slower in coming. The period of floating of the past three years has given world monetary leaders the time necessary to cope with the rapidly changing circumstances that have emerged. In fact, the float has allowed some new factors in the structure of monetary affairs to emerge. Fixed rate systems as we have known them don't seem to have worked well in our international environment recently, and we must conclude that their day has passed.

Assessing the Float

By the end of 1976, the world's major currencies had been floating for a period of more than three years and this arrangement began to look increasingly permanent. It is interesting to contrast the beginning of the float in 1973 with today. When the major currencies were allowed to float in 1973, it was considered an "interim measure." If the IMF-proposed change to its constitution as presented in Appendix C is ratified in 1977 or 1978, the float will finally be the legitimate monetary system. In all fairness, the float has helped the world through some very difficult economic and monetary times.

With the failure of the fixed rate systems of the Bretton Woods and Smithsonian agreements and the stormy and unstable history of the European joint float, there is little movement toward fixed rate systems currently. But what is the current feeling about the float, pro and con? On the pro side:

(1) Floating has worked during one of the most turbulent economic periods in monetary history. It has achieved a degree of stability.

(2) The floating system of the past three years has been hampered by governmental intervention and meddling and could have worked better left to market forces.

(3) The real economic problems today are rooted in the national economies of the major nations.

Until these are resolved no system will be able to work very well.

On the opposite side:

(1) Currency values can be volatile and are subject to manipulation.

(2) Floating has added new risks to international business transactions.

These are some of the commonly accepted conclusions about the float. Although they represent opinions, the float by the fall of 1976 had won the official praise of both the IMF and the U.S.

Lessons for
Today and Tomorrow

What does all this add up to? What can we learn from this recent five-year period of monetary affairs to help us with tomorrow?

If the floating is reasonably stable in the near future and if the IMF membership ratifies the Charter amendment, then there is very little likelihood that there will be any formal movement away from the floating and toward the adoption of either a gold standard, a fixed rate system, or a system of currency blocs. Of these, the main alternative to the floating is a system of currency blocs. But the stormy, short history of the European snake shows the kind of political and economic problems that are inherent in that kind of agreement. In fact, many wonder if the snake will continue. It appears that a world monetary system consisting of currency blocs is impractical in today's economic and political environment.

With a stable float, there is little need for the IMF to continue to hold negotiations on the form of the world monetary system. Instead, it will find its role changing with an increasing emphasis on the arrangement of credit facilities. These facilities would provide financial assistance for industrialized nations such as Italy and the United Kingdom with basic economic problems and for Third World nations with monetary problems associated with their energy bills. This is an important need and the IMF is the ideal organization to perform this service.

We can expect to see greater emphasis on international cooperation and voluntary coordination of national economies among the major industrialized nations. This will require more Rambouillet-type summit meetings. The main topics at these meetings will continue to be economic and trade-related rather than monetary.

The success of OPEC and the financial pressures on the Third World nations will spawn a number of attempts at establishing cartel arrangements, especially in the markets for basic commodities. Although a number of such negotiations are currently under way, it is unclear as to how successful they will be.

The basic assumption for these expectations is that the floating will continue with a reasonable degree of stability. If it does, it will contribute much toward the resolution of these international issues. But it is clear that many of the IMF nations have a basic preference for a fixed rate system. When these issues are resolved, it will be interesting to see if the IMF nations will then exercise their option in the Charter amendment and restore a fixed rate system. That could create another monetary muddle.

Appendix A

Foreign Exchange * and Price of Gold * *

January, 1972-December, 1976

1st Trading Day of Month

		Swiss FRANC	British POUND	West German MARK	French FRANC	Japanese YEN	GOLD**
1972	January	.2555	2.5550	.3060	.1925	.003190	44.38
	February	.2588	2.5995	.3128	.1965	.003235	48.10
	March	.2584	2.6063	.3145	.1981	.003310	48.20
	April	.2607	2.6170	.3158	.2048	.003295	48.41
	May	.2590	2.6112	.3147	.2056	.003300	50.35

*Foreign Exchange: Selling prices for bank transfers in the U.S. for payment abroad, afternoon quote (in dollars).

**London—Afternoon Fixings (in dollars).

Source: *The Wall Street Journal*

	Swiss FRANC	British POUND	West German MARK	French FRANC	Japanese YEN	GOLD**
June	.2608	2.6128	.3150	.2060	.003295	59.23
July	.2669	2.4190	.3178	.2108	.003340	66.00
August	.2651	2.4495	.3148	.2116	.003325	69.30
September	.2647	2.4488	.3136	.2078	.003326	66.85
October	.2628	2.4255	.3114	.2042	.003324	64.15
November	.2634	2.3565	.3124	.1996	.003325	64.00
December	.2656	2.3480	.3136	.1980	.003325	64.20
1973 January	.2652	2.3475	.3121	.1952	.003323	65.10
February	.2781	2.3880	.3174	.2003	.003326	66.60
March	.3230	2.5200	.3650	.2350	.003950	85.70
April	.3070	2.4780	.3520	.2203	.003800	89.25
May	.3087	2.4895	.3525	.2193	.003780	90.70
June	.3260	2.5730	.3745	.2320	.003800	117.75
July	.3465	2.5808	.4170	.2436	.003787	121.00
August	.3509	2.5191	.4270	.2400	.003810	117.50
September	.3308	2.4386	.4089	.2286	.003775	105.10
October	.3325	2.4152	.4152	.2315	.003770	96.75
November	.3230	2.4365	.4085	.2310	.003730	97.00
December	.3125	2.3415	.3810	.2140	.003600	100.25
1974 January	.3076	2.3225	.3702	.2055	.003580	112.25

	Swiss FRANC	British POUND	West German MARK	French FRANC	Japanese YEN	GOLD**
February	.3070	2.2710	.3616	.1970	.003360	130.50
March	.3173	2.2830	.3730	.2050	.003475	167.50
April	.3287	2.3970	.3932	.2089	.003577	174.10
May	.3407	2.4175	.4070	.2041	.003582	169.50
June	.3377	2.4010	.3982	.2055	.003533	155.50
July	.3330	2.3900	.3910	.2074	.003506	143.00
August	.3389	2.3835	.3886	.2136	.003341	159.40
September	.3331	2.3140	.3773	.2087	.003305	157.75
October	.3397	2.3372	.3781	.2116	.003355	155.75
November	.3506	2.3395	.3897	.2135	.003331	167.75
December	.3648	2.3253	.4006	.2160	.003331	185.75
1975 January	.3920	2.3362	.4154	.2252	.003326	175.00
February	.3963	2.3740	.4245	.2309	.003364	176.25
March	.4170	2.4355	.4396	.2409	.003506	181.85
April	.3971	2.4096	.4282	.2383	.003440	177.25
May	.3913	2.3481	.4206	.2421	.003424	166.00
June	.4020	2.3194	.4285	.2494	.003435	161.75
July	.3980	2.3030	.4320	.2465	.003384	166.50
August	.3711	2.1488	.3900	.2293	.003360	166.75
September	.3729	2.1105	.3876	.2273	.003359	149.25

	Swiss FRANC	British POUND	West German MARK	French FRANC	Japanese YEN	GOLD
October	.3698	2.0410	.3838	.2245	.003311	143.50
November	.3815	2.0760	.3916	.2301	.003317	143.25
December	.3749	2.0213	.3824	.2249	.003286	137.90
1976						
January	.3820	2.0249	.3820	.2237	.003280	140.35
February	.3871	2.0290	.3896	.2244	.003301	130.40
March	.3861	2.0232	.3875	.2228	.003317	132.30
April	.3959	1.8835	.3954	.2136	.003341	129.20
May	.3996	1.8275	.3944	.2146	.003347	128.35
June	.4128	1.7550	.3859	.2112	.003330	126.25
July	.4052	1.7925	.3882	.2110	.003367	122.90
August	.4037	1.7878	.3941	.2036	.003412	112.50
September	.4047	1.7755	.3968	.2031	.003467	105.70
October	.4086	1.6740	.4089	.2026	.003482	116.00
November	.4100	1.5960	.4151	.2004	.003384	122.60
December	.4078	1.6650	.4142	.2002	.003368	130.50

Appendix B

U.S. Trade and Payment Balances 1971-1976

Two national measures with great international significance mentioned throughout this book are the national balance of trade and balance of payments. They are simply defined as the net effect of imports and exports and the net flow of money into or out of a nation. Unfortunately, they are not so simply measured, nor is there agreement on how to measure them. To compound matters, the American approach differs from that of other nations. Also, the figures published in the United States are changed and revised frequently which further frustrates comparisons.

Presented on the following pages are three commonly used measures of the United States trade and payment balances for the period of 1971 through 1976.

Table 1
U.S. Trade and
Payment Balances, 1971-75
Quarterly, in Millions,
Seasonally Adjusted

	Trade Balance: Merchandise Trade Balance	Payment Balances: Current Account	Payment Balances: Basic Balance
1971	223	− 159	−1711
	− 755	− 933	−3163
	− 303	− 999	−3611
	−1433	−1790	−2155
1972	−1691	−2773	−3953
	−1597	−2608	−2338
	−1531	−2188	−2966
	−1590	−2131	−1855
1973	− 911	−1116	−1393
	− 231	− 849	−1085
	714	653	1917
	1383	1647	− 419
1974	− 123	26	1701
	−1459	−1787	−2302

	Trade Balance: Merchandise Trade Balance	Payment Balances: Current Account	Basic Balance
	−2315	−1500	−3574
	−1380	− 99	−6529
1975	1495	1698	− 977
	3274	3753	982
	2111	3446	1396
	2165	3017	− 4

Source: U.S. Department of Commerce, Bureau of Economic Analysis, "Survey of Current Business," June, 1975, p. 29, and March, 1976, p. 39.

Table 2
U.S. Trade and Payment Balances, 1976
Monthly, in
Millions, Seasonally Adjusted

	Trade Balances: Merchandise	Census	Payment Balance: Current Account
January	− 73		
February	− 141		
March	− 651		
First Quarter	−1510	− 864	− 60
April	− 202		
May	396		
June	− 377		
Second Quarter	−1340	− 184	816
July	− 827		
August	− 758		
September	− 779		
Third Quarter	−3110	−2380	−729
October	− 696		

	Trade Balances: Merchandise	Census	Payment Balance: Current Account
November	−1030		
December	− 610		
Fourth Quarter	−3250	−2140	− 817
1976 Totals*	−9560	−5870	−604

Merchandise Trade Balance, Balance of Payments Basis: excludes military trade and includes other adjustments.

Merchandise Trade Balance, Census Basis: includes military trade and excludes certain other adjustments. The more widely watched balance.

Balance of Payments, Current Account Basis: includes merchandise trade, trade in services, and unilateral transfers such as aid grants and pensions to Americans living abroad.

Source: *The Wall Street Journal.*

*Will not agree due to rounding.

The interpretation and use of trade and payment information have changed recently; surpluses were regarded as "good," and deficits as "bad". In a fixed rate world monetary system, the trade and payment balances of a nation were often valid indicators of the relative soundness of the par value of the currency. Usually, the existence of a continued and large trade or payment deficit meant that the currency was weak and would eventually be devalued. However, in a floating system, the relationship between these balances and the value of a currency is less direct and clear.

Some dissent has been voiced that surpluses are good. Occasionally, the editors of the *Journal* would speak to this subject. When the world is considered as a whole, the existence of surpluses in some nations means that deficits must exist in others. The real goal of international trade should be economic efficiency rather than some nations producing larger trade surpluses than others. In fact, many of the actions that a nation can take to improve its trade position can be interpreted by other nations as "protectionist" and they in turn will take similar actions. If such a sequence of events continues, it could result in a trade war and free trade would be destroyed. Thus, the proper analysis of trade and payment balances should adopt this world viewpoint and consider these international factors.

A very big change in the measurement and reporting of U.S. trade and payment information occurred in 1976. It began in 1974 when the Advisory Committee on the Presentation of Balance of Payment Statistics was assembled to consider the U.S. trade and payment balances. Late in 1975, the panel recommended that the U.S. discontinue reporting some traditionally emphasized "bottom line" figures (balances) which it believed were now meaningless and misleading. The following two reasons were given to support this recommendation:

(1) Since the floating of currencies in 1973, some of the trade and payment balances had lost the significance they had under the fixed rate system.

(2) The increased complexity of international financial flows, especially those related to OPEC nations, had made some of the concepts obsolete. Instead, the committee recommended that data on international transactions be presented without the traditional emphasis of certain figures. The trade balances would be retained, however.

As might be expected, this move was controversial and criticized by those who felt that the "old balances" did tell some interesting things even under the current monetary system.

In May, 1976, the U.S. government adopted most of the recommendations of the advisory panel and announced that it would stop publishing three major measures of the U.S. balance of payments: the basic balance, the official reserve balance and the net liquidity balance. Instead, approximately six weeks after the end of each quarter, the Commerce Department would release data on imports and exports, U.S. assets abroad and foreign assets in the United States and call it "Selected Data on International Transactions of the United States." Four weeks later, in a report titled, "Summary of U.S. International Transactions," four partial balances would be presented: merchandise trade; goods and services; goods, services, and remittances; and the current account balance. Still later, the Commerce Department would publish additional data on these items in its monthly "Survey of Current Business." All interested parties should be able to use this information to compute the old basic and official reserve balances for themselves, according to the announcement.

Starting with the June, 1976 issue of "Survey of Current Business," trade and payment information about the United States is presented in a new format, emphasizing the following figures:

Exports of goods and services; Transfers of goods and services under U.S. military grant programs, net; Imports of goods and services; U.S. military grants of goods and services, net; Unilateral transfers, net; U.S. assets abroad, net; Foreign assets in the U.S., net; and Memoranda.

The merchandise trade balance and balance on current account are still provided at the bottom of the table in the Memoranda section. The U.S. Department of Commerce has gone back to 1960 and restated all trade and payment information to conform to this new presentation format.

Appendix C

Details of Proposed Amendment

To IMF Charter, Article IV

"Obligations Regarding

Exchange Arrangements"

Keystone of New IMF Accord
Represents Broad Changes
In Language, Philosophy

By Charles N. Stabler

KINGSTON, Jamaica—Flexible instead of rigid. Pragmatic rather than ideological. Adaptable as opposed to cumbersome. And without gold as a common denominator.

Thus, in these broad terms, does the new Article IV proposed for amendment to the basic document of the 128-member International

Monetary Fund differ from the currently discredited rule on exchange-rate adjustments adopted in 1944, when the fund was born at Bretton Woods, N.H.

Article IV, titled "Obligations Regarding Exchange Arrangements," was the keystone of the package finally agreed upon. Considering its long-term significance, the proposed amendment generated little argument.

The words are often vague and subject to varying interpretations. As some of the delegates emphasized, how this agreement or any other agreement among sovereign nations works in practice will depend on the willingness to cooperate in good faith and on the benefits outweighing the drawbacks.

But the agreement will affect for some years to come how nations manage their financial dealings with each other, what they pay for imports, and employment levels in their export industries. Therefore, while the proposed amendment itself doesn't contain any surprises, its specific wording is worth a close look.

Basic Objective

The basic objective of the new system isn't substantively different from the old. The new Section 1 says: "The essential purpose of the international monetary system is to provide a framework that facilitates the exchange of goods, services and capital among countries, and that sustains sound economic growth. . . . A principal objective is the continuing development of the orderly underlying conditions that are necessary for financial and economic stability."

To promote a stable system of exchange rates, the members will make several key commitments.

Each country will "direct its economic and financial policies toward the objective of fostering orderly economic growth with reasonable price stability, with due regard to its circumstances." Also, the country will "seek to promote stability by fostering orderly underlying economic and financial conditions and a monetary system that doesn't tend to produce erratic disruptions."

These provisions reflect the view that orderly exchange markets are the result of orderly underlying economic conditions. They imply that domestic money managers will have to pay closer attention to foreign-exchange markets when setting policy. The "due regard to circumstances" clause is to accommodate some less-developed countries that have firmly retrenched inflationary forces.

"Clean Float"

There is a provision for a "clean float." It requires countries "to avoid manipulating exchange rates or the international monetary system in order to prevent effective balance-of-payments adjustment or to gain an unfair competitive advantage over other members."

Accommodating the French view, the article provides that a nation may establish a par value for its currency, but it won't be in terms of gold. The par value may be set in relation to Special Drawing Rights, an IMF bookkeeping entry called "paper gold" and itself valued in terms of a group of other currencies.

To set a par value the country must have the concurrence of the fund, through its executive directors. The country must agree to maintain its par value, by some type of intervention in the market, so that it doesn't fluctuate outside a top-to-bottom band of 4.5%, "or by such other margin as the fund may adopt by an 85% majority."

A change in a par value may be proposed to correct "or prevent the emergence of" fundamental disequilibrium. This is a more flexible rule than Bretton Woods provided, allowing quicker reaction to changed economic conditions.

If a country wants to abandon its par value it may do so by notifying the fund. But, by an 85% majority, the fund may object. If the member goes ahead anyhow, it becomes subject to the standard sanctions of loss of credit facilities and, ultimately, expulsion from the agency.

Par-Rate System

As for general restoration of a par-rate system, as desired by the French and some other nations, the amendment says this: "The fund may determine by an 85% majority of the total voting power that international economic conditions permit the introduction of a widespread system of exchange arrangements based on stable but adjustable par values."

The significance of the 85% majority requirement is that the U.S. has voting power of about 20%. Therefore, the U.S. could veto the restoration of a par-value system. Or, if the U.S. should adopt a par value and later wish to drop it, the move couldn't be vetoed by other countries.

If a nation wants to let its currency float, as the U.S. currently does, it still is subject to surveillance by the fund and to other conditions. "The fund shall exercise firm surveillance over the exchange-rate policies of members and shall adopt specific principles for the guidance of all members with respect to those policies. Each member shall provide the fund with information necessary for such surveillance," says the amendment.

This means the members must keep the fund informed of domestic economic monetary policy, because domestic policy affects a nation's foreign-exchange rate. But it doesn't give the fund any power to set or alter the domestic policies of its members.

A floating-rate country also is generally obligated to intervene on foreign-exchange markets to offset disorderly or erratic conditions that aren't caused by underlying economic factors. But how this obligation will work in practice remains to be seen. For example, there isn't any certain way to determine if an exchange-rate movement is "erratic" or does reflect real economic change.

On this score, says Edwin H. Yeo, U.S. Treasury Under Secretary for Monetary Affairs, "We agreed to broaden and deepen contacts among our central banks through fuller discussion and exchange of information."

The future role of gold also can't be pre-

dicted with certainty. Largely at the urging
of the U.S., it has been banished from the
structure set up by the amendment. But
whether the metal will depart so obligingly
from the monetary picture remains to be seen.

Under the package agreement, the IMF
will be auctioning off part of its gold holdings. Central banks will be able to buy gold,
although they won't be buying it directly
from the IMF. Some, perhaps France, are
expected to add to their reserve holdings of
the metal.

In this and other ways, it is likely that
market forces will dictate how the new articles will work in the real economic world.

Text Index